SUNIL GUPTA

The Tate Photography Series is a celebration of international and British photography in the Tate collection and an introduction to some of the most significant photographers at work today. Previous sets of four in the series have explored the themes of Community and Solidarity, and Ecology and Environment.

Each book focuses on an individual photographer and features a specially selected sequence of photographs, an introduction by a Tate curator and a conversation with, or statement by, the artist. These collaborative books as dialogues between artists and experts aim to enrich our understanding of photography and its connection to everyday life, and collectively they move from city streets to seashores, across landscapes and subcultures, through identities and interiors, in a visual travelogue of our world today.

The theme for Series Three is Queer and Visible, bringing together four artists who use photography to unfold valuable insights into queer life. Each artist uniquely reflects upon societal constructs of sexuality and race, and responds to the experience of living in a predominantly white and heteronormative society.

To see and to make seen, to work in good faith, to produce artful storytelling and resonant images – these are the qualities we seek from good photography. The artist-photographer notices and captures, calls for a moment of our divided and hurried attention, and reveals connection and pattern, emotion and meaning. The work sets out to expand the possible and make hearts and minds more spacious.

Series Three

3:1 **LAURA AGUILAR**
3:2 **SUNIL GUPTA**
3:3 **LYLE ASHTON HARRIS**
3:4 **AJAMU X**

SUNIL GUPTA

Edited by
Jasmine Kaur Chohan

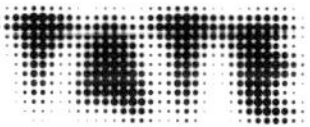

First published 2025 by order of the Tate Trustees
by Tate Publishing, a division of Tate Enterprises Ltd,
Millbank, London SW1P 4RG
www.tate.org.uk/publishing

A catalogue record for this book is available from the British Library

ISBN 978 1 84976 955 6

Distributed in the United States and Canada
by ABRAMS, New York

Library of Congress Control Number applied for

Series Editor: Simon Armstrong
Senior Editor: Nicola Bion
Production: Bill Jones
Picture Research: Roz Hill
Designed by Sarah Boris
Colour reproduction by Westerham Press, London
Printed and bound in the UK by Westerham Press, London

Front cover: *Fakroon* 1974, from the series Friends and Lovers: Coming Out in the 1970s, Montreal
Back cover top: *Rizwan, Delhi* 2015 from the series Dissent and Desire
Back cover bottom: *Gay* 1986, from the series Black Experience, London

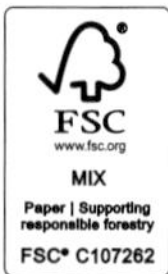

CONTENTS

INTRODUCTION

Sunil Gupta is now revered as one of the most influential photographers on the British and global contemporary art scene, but this was not always the case. For decades, he has been working as a photographer, curator, educator and policymaker to increase visibility for both the queer and politically Black communities.

Gupta was born into an atypical Indian family in Delhi in 1953. His father, a landowner from Uttar Pradesh, and his mother, a Tibetan migrant who was brought up by a British Protestant woman in Amritsar, married against his paternal family's will and lived a cosmopolitan life in New Delhi. Gupta's sexual and aesthetic awakening began in Delhi, where the heat allowed for loose clothing and play, and the vibrance of Bollywood was ever-present.

Using Bollywood stills as a visual reference, he began photographing his family and friends, who became a staple in his work, depicted in series such as Friends & Lovers Coming Out in Montreal in the 1970s (1971–82) and Lovers: Ten Years On (1984). In series such as Exiles (1986–7) or Reflections of the Black Experience (1986), he still used his friends posing as actors to protect the identity of those he had met.

At fifteen, Gupta's family migrated to Montreal, Canada, where he discovered a verbal and theoretical language that allowed him to define his identity as a gay man and explore his photographic practice. Studying for a B'Comm at Concordia University, Montreal, he threw himself into the Gay Liberation Movement. Working for a university newspaper was his first foray into publishing his work, but his role as an activist truly defined his photographic practices.

Moving to New York in 1976, Gupta flourished both photographically and sexually. In the 1970s, being gay was celebrated in the city, and his artistic capabilities were fostered by people like Lisette Model at the New School. One of Gupta's most popular series, Christopher Street, New York (1976), came out of this epoch of liberation. These intimate, black-and-white photographs of gay people on the streets of New York allowed him to use his camera to strike up conversations and immerse himself in the community.

Gupta followed his partner, Rudy Leuthold, from New York to London, gaining his diploma in photography at West Surrey College of Art and Design in Farnham and studying for his MA at the Royal College of

Art, London. The queer community in the UK was then under attack through policies such as Section 28 (1988), and the AIDS epidemic had reached London, villainising an entire sector of society. As a result, Gupta's work became even more political. Series such as 'Pretended' Family Relationships (1988) combined his photographs of protest and posed friends with accompanying poems by his then-partner Stephen Dodd. The impact of Gupta's HIV-positive diagnosis is evident in *Ecstatic Antibodies* (1990), a pro-sex and pro-queer exhibition he curated with Tessa Boffin to counter the British government's response to HIV.

Experiencing the hypervisibility of ethnic minority communities in the UK and attacks by the extreme right, Gupta's Indian identity became increasingly important in his work. Gupta, alongside Monika Baker, Merle Van den Bosch, Armet Francis, Michael Jess, George Shire and Lance Watson, were the founding members of the photography group Autograph, known then as the Association of Black Photographers (ABP). Between 1988 and 2007, Autograph functioned as an agency, initiating projects and influencing policy and practice, showcasing alternative models for creating and sharing work.

Gupta's time in London was a tale of two cities. Initially, he made great strides in exhibiting his work and impacting policy changes in the arts, but the politically Black arts movement ran out of steam in the late 1990s and opportunities were drying up. At fifty years old, in 2004, Gupta returned to India to help 'try and fix things there'. The activist spirit in him was reinvigorated by the bold LGBTQ community in New Delhi. Works from Mr Malhotra's Party (2007–12) reflect his real subjects gazing directly into the camera, counteracting the absence of the direct gaze in the Exiles series.

In 2012, due to the increasingly anti-LGBTQ atmosphere, Gupta moved with his partner Charan Singh back to London. The duo have since been collaborating on numerous projects such as Dissent and Desire (2015) and Lovers Revisited (ongoing).

Gupta holds a mirror up to society, forcing us to see those who have been made invisible. His work can be described in many ways, but most immediately, it can be seen as an exploration and understanding of identity, sexual and political agency, one's community, and one's self.

Jasmine Kaur Chohan
Assistant Curator, Contemporary British Art, Tate Britain

SUNIL GUPTA AND JASMINE CHOHAN IN CONVERSATION

Jasmine Chohan:

What was the reason behind your move from India to Canada, and what was it like?

Sunil Gupta:

I think my mother was probably the bigger driving force [of my parents]. She was slightly more unusual in the Indian context. My dad was very typical: a feudal guy from Uttar Pradesh, he was not inclined to move – I mean his entire reason to exist was around him. Nobody asked me [anything], they just told me that we were going, and so I think for me it was an adventure. I was having quite a good time where I was.

My mother was Protestant and she had a very mixed background. She was, we think, a Tibetan migrant worker's child, who was left behind and then adopted by a British woman who moved her to Amritsar. She had her schooling in Amritsar. It was in Urdu, and she did her college [work] in Lahore and Canada, also in English. She wasn't Hindi speaking in that sense, but my dad was. His family weren't thrilled about her because she was Christian and not like them and didn't appear to have any family of her own. We were kind of a nuclear family, which was unusual at the time. There were just the four of us – I have a sibling – and we had these cousins who came from the region to visit who seemed completely different, you know, who were not urban.

Anyway, one parent put me on the plane to the other parent who had gone earlier, and I thought it would be all very exciting and would feel like being in a movie. What I knew of contemporary North America was through the cinema, and it did look like that at first. I'd never been anywhere like that where it was really clean. The streets and the pavements were really straight, and the pavements were really clear of anything and there were clearly demarcated boundaries. That was the pavement, and there was the road, and there was the building, and the building met the pavement in a straight line. We don't have that in India, so that was kind of a novelty.

JC In previous interviews you have mentioned that the first moment you were drawn to cameras was in India after watching Bollywood films. Could you explain a little bit more about your relationship to photography, when the interest started, and how it developed?

SG Our cultural exposure was largely to cinema. We weren't a family that went to museums. My mum was a movie fan, so there were some Western movies, but there was obviously a lot of Bollywood. That's what I grew up with: big Bollywood blockbusters – colourful, all-singing and dancing. It was like a big event with participation, almost operatic.

Then there was the camera in the family. My father took family snaps occasionally and he would leave a camera lying around. When we became teenagers I became more interested in it, and I had a sister who was willing to be a model. She was four years older. She had teenage-girl magazines from the West and a couple of Indian ones, so we would emulate that kind of look.

My friend and I started to develop films at home in a very rudimentary fashion. Everything was against it – the climate, the temperature – but we tried. He also had some sisters who were willing to pose, so we had a proper go at it.

When we arrived in Montreal, photography became a hobby. I did part-time work as a kid, so I could suddenly afford to buy an analogue camera. I could take photos and, with the suitable climate, I could process them at home and it did work.

JC So, from the very beginning you did a lot of your printing at home.

SG Yes, in my loo! I bought an enlarger for $150. I was really interested in making prints, so I taught myself through the Time-Life series of books which are called The Print and The Negative, among others. They're very good guides with great pictures. Both the content and the technique were accessible, so I taught myself that way, but I had no ambition to pursue it seriously. Even in Montreal there was no photography scene, so it remained a hobby until I found an unexpected audience through my involvement with the gay student society at university. They decided to publish a newsletter and wanted pictures, so I volunteered to take them. I became the photographer, and seeing my work in print gave me an audience.

JC It's really interesting to see that your subject matter remained quite consistent from the very beginning of your practice. There's a clear focus on family and friends and a form of documentary photography.

SG Yes, it came together in a weird kind of unplanned way. I think if I hadn't left India, neither the photography nor being gay would have happened.

JC Where did your sexual awakening occur and where did you fully embrace your identity as a gay man?

SG It all happened in India. Indians live in these big, extended families, and everything is very physical. People don't sit around in sitting rooms in armchairs having a chat; they lie on top of each other. If you ever see an Indian social occasion, they're all over each other casually – it's very touchy-feely.

JC But was it still quite a closeted experience in India?

SG You couldn't talk about it – you didn't have the language to do so. I never knew what gay meant because what I did wasn't called gay. I don't think it was called anything. People just had fun.

JC Sexuality was more of a fluid notion?

SG Yes, but there was no language. That was the unfortunate thing. There was no way to talk about it, just that you knew that you definitely weren't going to mention anything like it to your parents or at proper parties.

JC But then that changed when you went to Montreal?

SG Totally. Being university-based, the language was really full and flowing and academic. Studies were being done and I quickly became very literate in what being gay meant. It was very politicised. I saw it as an innovative political framework and it became a tool to stand up to the family and capitalism, which seemed to be in bed with one another. They need each other.

JC So your identity as a gay man went hand in hand with your identity as an activist?

SG Yes, because we genuinely believed that it was slightly revolutionary to not marry, not reproduce, not buy a house, not get a mortgage, not acquire things like cars and have children who need more things and more houses. That's what happens to families – they get involved in this ever-expanding acquisition of things and capital.

JC After Montreal, you made your way to New York. What prompted that move?

SG I followed Rudy Leuthold who got a job there. New York turned out to be the centre of photography in a way I had never experienced before. There were heaps of photography galleries, which I had never seen in Canada or India. All the museums were showing photography of some kind, some with permanently displayed collections from the history of photography.

I was ostensibly in New York doing an MBA. However, I got sucked into the photo world, meeting people and getting drawn into auctions, seeing original work in a way I'd only seen in reproduction before – actual vintage prints. I decided to drop out of my MBA and discovered photography courses you could attend.

New York was also the centre of gay liberation between Stonewall and the mid-1970s, and hundreds or thousands of young gay men had moved to New York to get away from conservative Christian family environments in the US. They were very visible in public, unlike my gay life which had only happened at night in nightclubs. Christopher Street was full of gay men day and night, something entirely new to me.

New York was a positive reinforcement towards my interest in both gay life and photography. I did courses with Lisette Model and two others at the New School, and if I had to name someone who influenced me towards photography over business, it would be her. My parents were horrified; they had visions of me in a suit making lots of money in the city, not living in jeans and dragging a camera bag around the world. They saw photography as a working-class trade, like wedding photography. But my mind was set then.

JC A lot of the images from the series Christopher Street, New York 1976 are of people that you casually come across in the streets, and it has a documentary/street photography style. In comparison, in the series Exiles (1986–7), photographed in India, the people are posed and often actors or friends. What perpetuated this transition from documentary photography on the streets, and fleeting moments, to staged photographs? And do you think that then became a bit of a staple in your photography?

SG It coincided with the period when I was still a student, between 1980 and 1983. On the one hand, I thought I wanted to be a humanist documentary photographer. My heroes were people like W. Eugene Smith, who focused on heavy-duty social issues and social justice narratives through photography. But in India, the issue of being gay wasn't openly discussed. People weren't willing to be photographed with that label. So, while I could have documented it, showing such work would have been awkward and potentially harmful to those involved.

This posed a problem for my documentary methodology. I was facing a crisis about how to approach this subject sensitively. My photographic style was largely self-taught, influenced by American East Coast modernist photographers like Robert Frank, Lee Friedlander and Diane Arbus.

When I created Exiles, I aimed for authenticity in the locations and the people – real gay Indians. Everything about the setting and subjects was authentic, except the narrative constructed in the photographs. This blurred the lines of reality for documentary work, causing some viewers to feel misled when they discovered the images weren't entirely real.

JC That constructed documentary style imagery seems to come to the fore when you moved here to London. It comes up in series like Reflections of the Black Experience 1986. Do you think the focal point of your identity shifted when moving to London, from being a gay man to being a gay person of colour?

SG Oh, that's easy. So my life in Canada and New York was kind of personally devoid of race. My Indianness was a non-issue because people there had never heard of it. My ethnicity didn't seem to hinder me from doing what I wanted, like getting jobs or dating. However, when I came to England, I realised that I was part of a visible minority group that was disliked by some people, and I experienced some blatant racism which I wasn't accustomed to. Once on the tube, someone told me, 'I think you should go home,' and I misunderstood, thinking he meant my apartment, and I said, 'but I've just come from there'. More troubling incidents followed; my sister was chased by skinheads in Shepherd's Bush. It made me aware of the racial issues prevalent in society.

In the early 1980s, during a post-colonial moment, I encountered Indian-origin theorists like Homi Bhabha, who discussed post-colonial theory. At art school in London, there were very few Indians and a few Afro-Caribbeans, and we naturally gravitated towards each other. In 1983, we organised one of the earliest black student shows at the RCA. It was a separate exhibition from the regular degree shows, held in a room we requested in the Darwin Building near Hyde Park. This led us to engage with the Greater London Council (GLC) and their Race Equality Unit, where I met Parminder Vir, who headed the unit. This period was transformative for me politically. I became disillusioned with the commercial art world and instead got involved with the GLC, where I became an unpaid advisor on anti-racist policies. We worked with Ken Livingstone and influenced advertising policies to address racial stereotypes. I became more involved with organisations like the Arts Council and London Arts, focusing on policy and advocating for change through structured frameworks.

My work didn't pay much, if any, money. So, I also ended up working for Fleet Street to make a living. Photography became my day job, shooting for hire. I worked for magazines and newspapers doing editorial work. That's how I sustained myself for a while.

JC And so did those photographs that you were taking for Fleet Street make their way into your work, like 'Pretended' Family Relationships (1988)?

SG Some of the aesthetics and the portraits were a big part of my work. I had to buy a second-hand larger-format camera for the commercial assignments, which I could then use for my personal portraits. My technique became more driven by the marketplace and I had to maintain a level of perfection for the jobs. I got a bit obsessed with making perfect pictures, perfect exposures, and all that.

However, the excitement of seeing my name in publications like The Times began to wane. I realised I was just contributing to a giant machine over which I had no control. I couldn't dictate how my photos were used or the narratives they would support – the captions were always written for me. The media outlets had their own perspectives and agendas that weren't going to change easily.

JC A lot of your photographs revolve around these constructed family relationships that you have. Could you speak about what those communities mean to you, and how and why they've become such an integral part of your photography?

SG Well, I was interested in homosexual relationships more than I was interested in the sex part of homosexuality, which was heavily covered in the gay media. Emerging gay photographers like Robert Mapplethorpe were very focused on the body, but that was of less interest to me. In my experience as a gay man, sex was often straightforward and not a problem, but forming and maintaining relationships was challenging. This was especially true back then when societal barriers made it difficult to live together, formalise relationships or secure basic rights like joint ownership or inheritance. When AIDS emerged, it highlighted how vulnerable these relationships were legally – surviving partners could lose everything to blood relatives. The personal trigger for exploring these themes in my work came when my own relationship ended unexpectedly. This event, coupled with the political climate of Clause 28 which targeted 'pretend families', motivated me to create art around these issues.

JC I just wanted to talk a little bit about you moving back to India from London. What triggered that move?

SG Well, there were a couple of reasons for my move to India. The unofficial version is that I met a guy there and decided to go for it. The official version is more about turning fifty, realising I had no work, being HIV positive, and feeling like everything I was trying to do had run out of steam. The Black Arts movement was fading, and the Young British Artists (YBAs) were rising, but I was older and financially struggling. I had a big farewell party in London, where I bluntly stated my reasons for leaving, saying to everyone, 'you're racist and homophobic'.

Being in India turned out to be another serendipitous twist. There wasn't much happening in photography or the gay scene, which motivated me to get involved. I joined a queer activist group, helped organise cultural events, and found a gallery willing to work with me on photography – a rarity in a country without state funding or grants. I embarked on a significant research project, exploring contemporary Indian photography in four major cities, which eventually led to exhibitions and recognition. Vadehra Art Gallery in

Delhi took a chance on representing me and even published a monograph entitled Queer, a groundbreaking move for them. In Delhi, things changed when I met someone new. We decided to move back to London, where we could blend in more easily as just another desi couple. The move was partly driven by social class differences in India, where acceptance among my liberal friends was a challenge. Now, in London, life is simpler.

JC Could we just touch on Lovers: Ten Years On 1984, and then Lovers Revisited (ongoing). What made you want to revisit the series?

SG Well, principally because one of the original couples wanted to have a new picture. The new partner felt upset because the original picture had become famous on a postcard made by Tate. She had been buying them up and sticking her face on the other one's face and sending them around. We did a new picture and realised one photo wouldn't suffice, so we decided to create a whole series and publish it as a mini book. The series features people we know, it's not a comprehensive study.

Over the forty years between them, interesting differences and contrasts have emerged. To distinguish the new ones, we shot them in colour and made them very large and high-resolution, around 5 feet tall. The landscape has changed. Now, nobody identifies as just gay or lesbian; everyone identifies as queer or gender fluid. Some couples in the series even consist of three people. There's more diversity in age, with younger and older participants. Because we travel extensively for our work, we've included people from various places – London, New York, Australia, Lisbon, Paris, Milan and even India. The response has been varied; some wanted a formal portrait while others wanted something more casual. Overall, the series feels more contemporary and vibrant than the first one. Each new addition brings something different, which enriches the series.

JC Finally, in your work Homelands in 2000 you took photographs in Canada, India and England to explore a concept of home. Is the work reflective of your identity as being hyphenated?

SG It's complicated, but on one level, being Canadian is the easiest thing. Everyone thinks Canadians are wonderful, so I'm quite happy with that non-exciting category. When I returned to live in India in the 2000s, teaching, making art and engaging in activism, I felt somewhat special because I believed India needed action. Any person of Indian origin who wants to contribute positively should do so. I thought of my work as a calling. Why am I here writing Arts Council documents to make England look better? I should be in India, writing documents for an Indian Arts Council (even though it doesn't exist) to help those who need it more than people here. Yes, in that sense, I felt more nationalistic. I don't feel nationalistic here [in the UK] at all. On the other hand, I've seen too much nationalism in India. What seems like a calling can also be a lot of flag-waving.

When I land in Delhi or Montreal, I immediately recognise the smell of petrol in Montreal or the pollution in Delhi. They are familiar to me, so I can function well. Including London, yeah.

Ultimately, I feel internationalised. I'm happiest in a non-specific nationality situation. I feel most comfortable among people in various diasporas. I don't feel like I have one specific home; everywhere is home and nowhere is home.

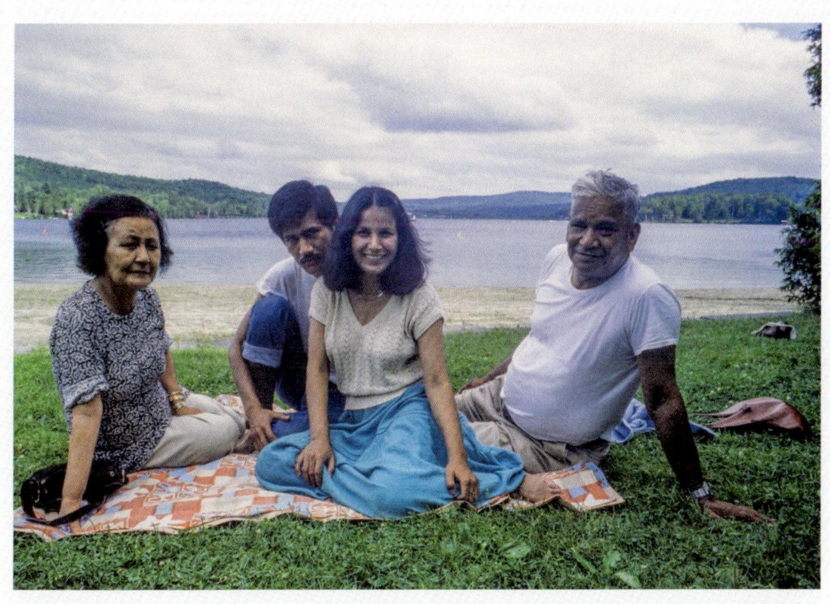

Social Security, Untitled #13, Montreal c.1972 (from left to right: Penny, Sunil, Shalini, Ram)

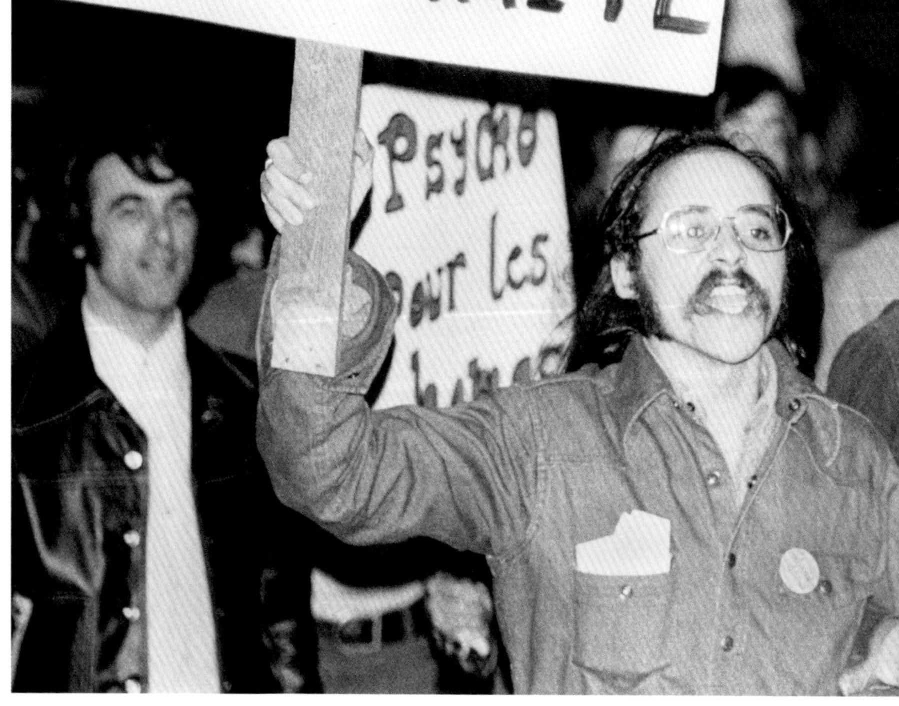
TRAVAILLEURS
GAIS
SOLIDARITÉ

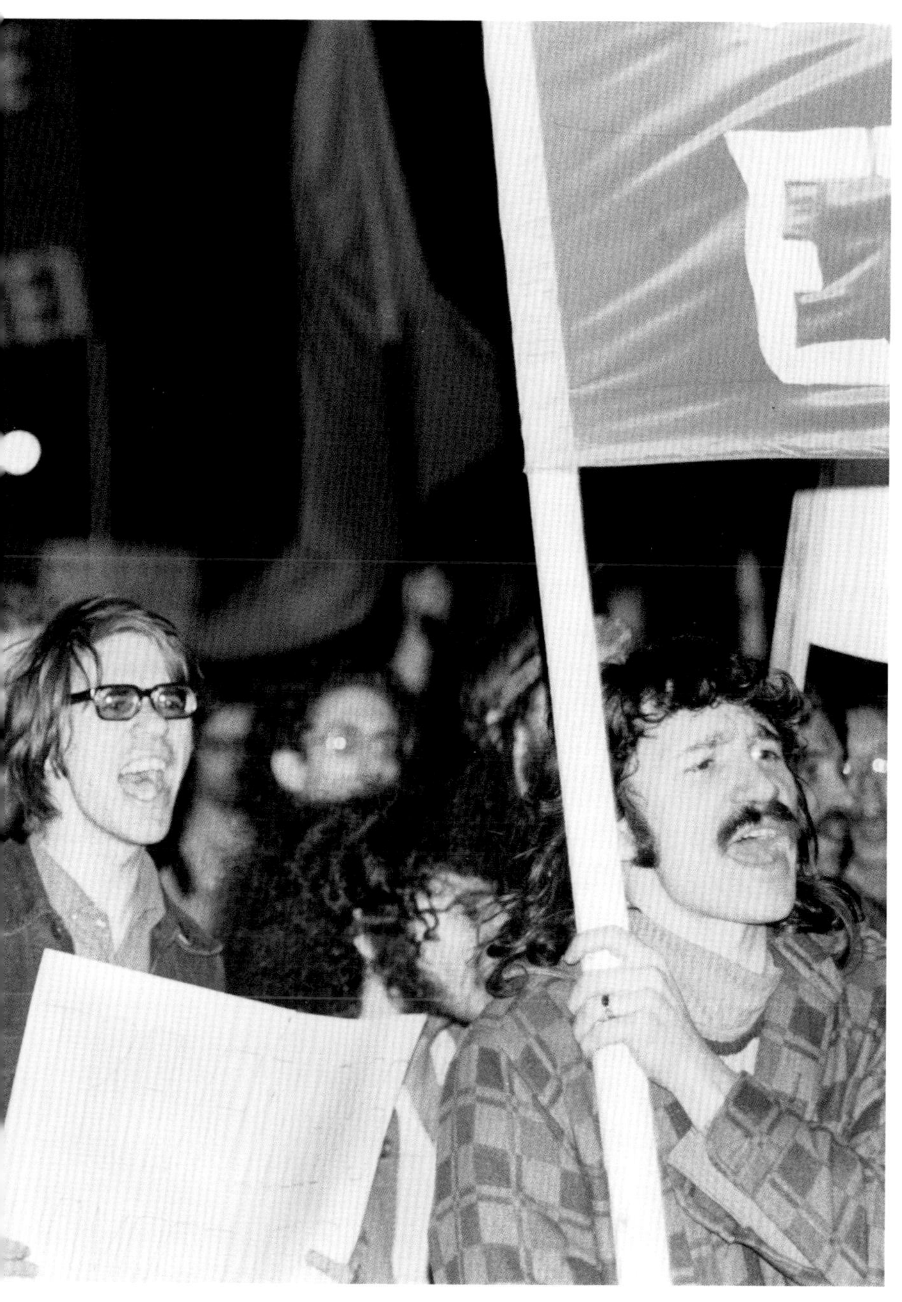

Gay Liberation demonstrators join workers rally on May Day, Montreal c.1972, from the series Friends and Lovers: Coming Out in the 1970s, Montreal

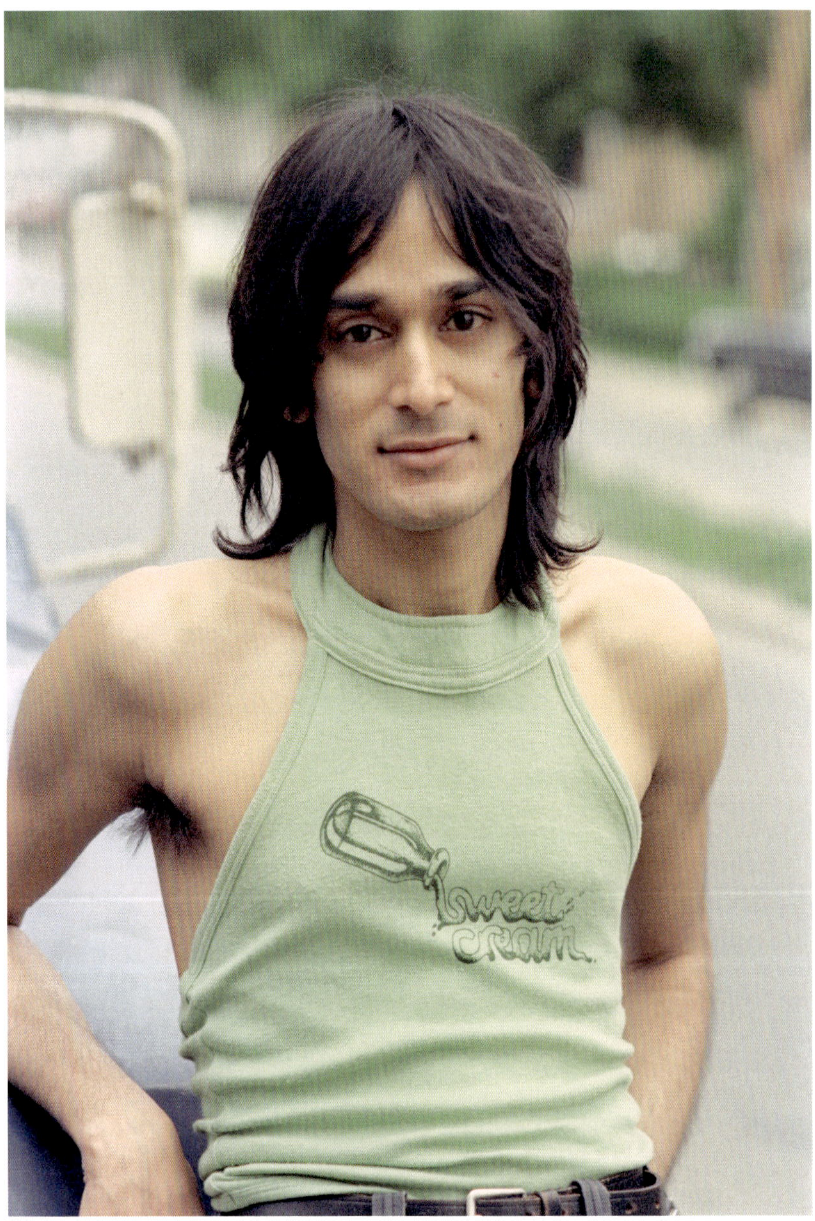

Fakroon 1974, from the series Friends and Lovers: Coming Out in the 1970s, Montreal

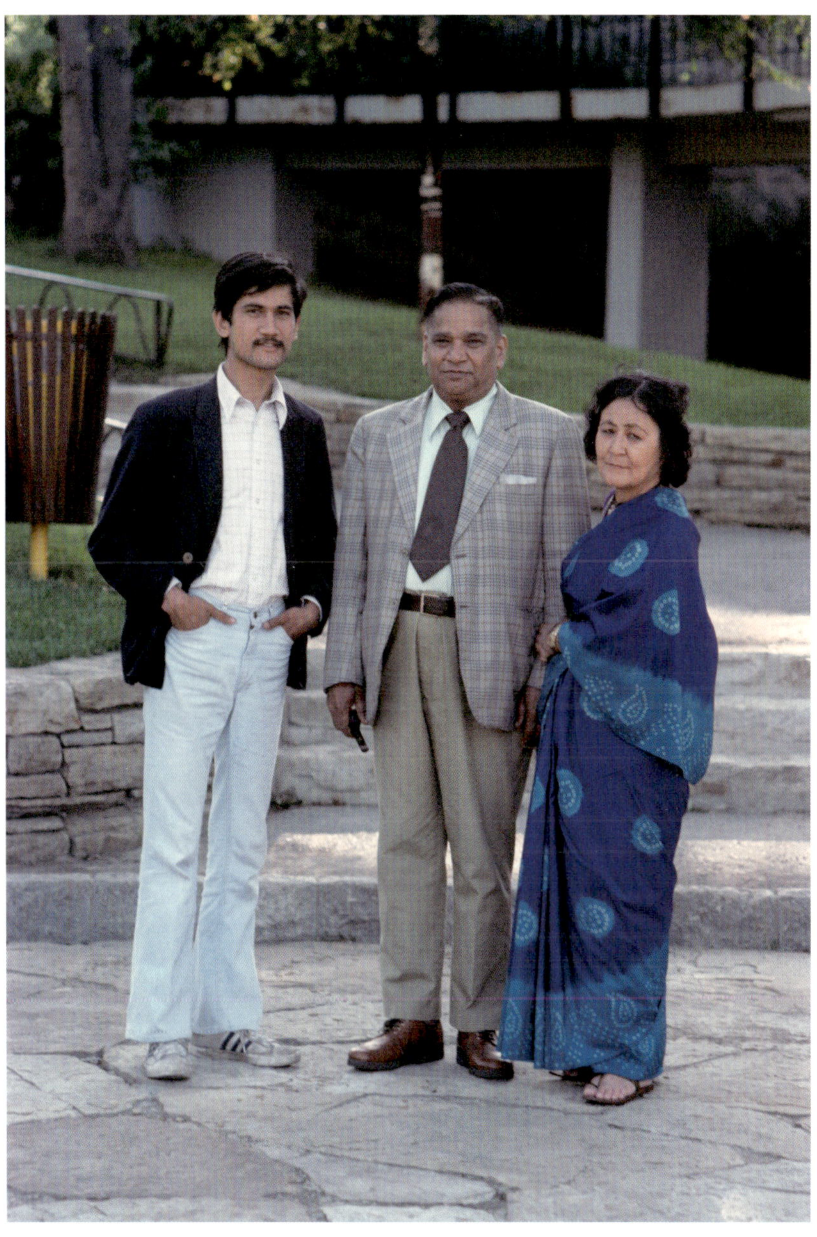

Sunil and his parents, Shri Ram and Penny Gupta 1975, from the series Friends and Lovers: Coming Out in the 1970s, Montreal

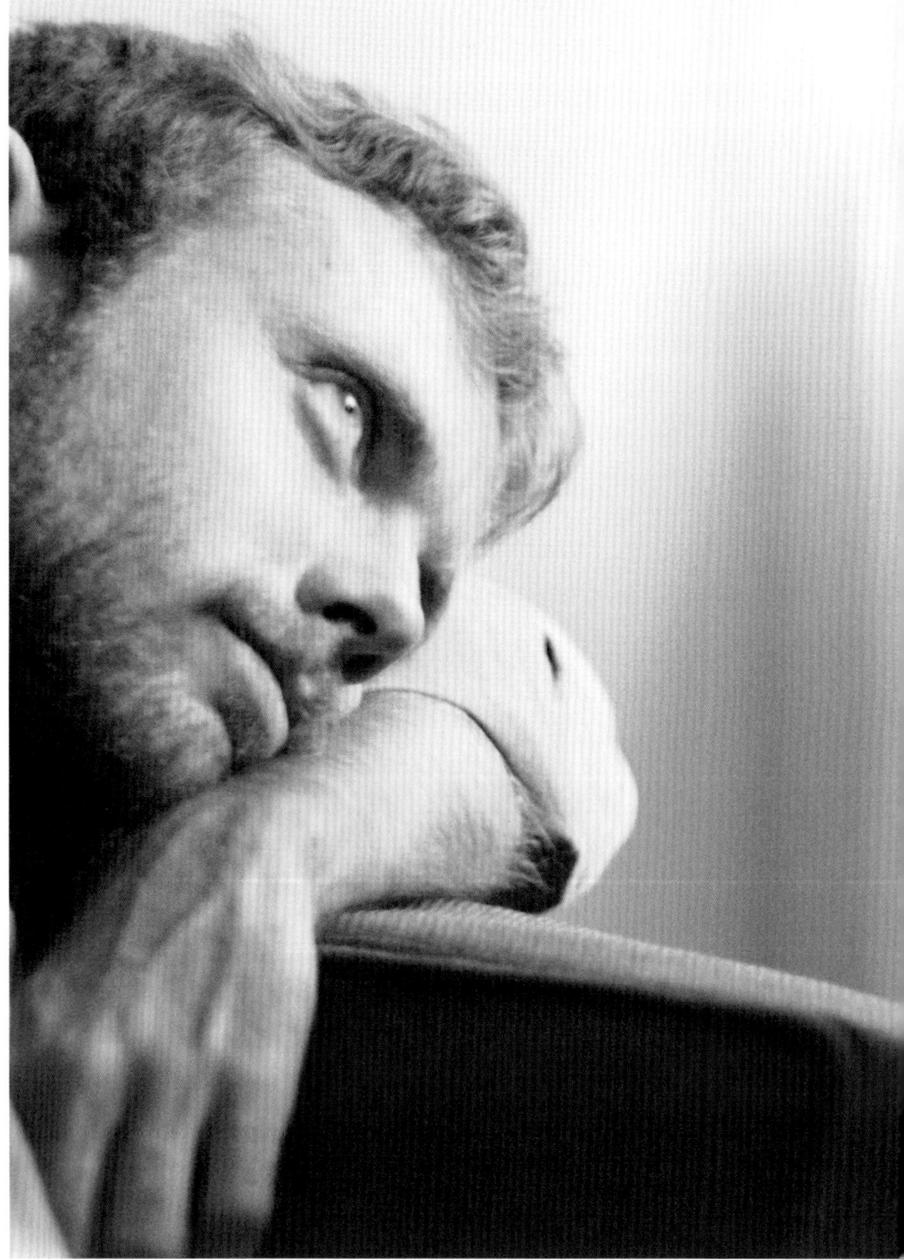

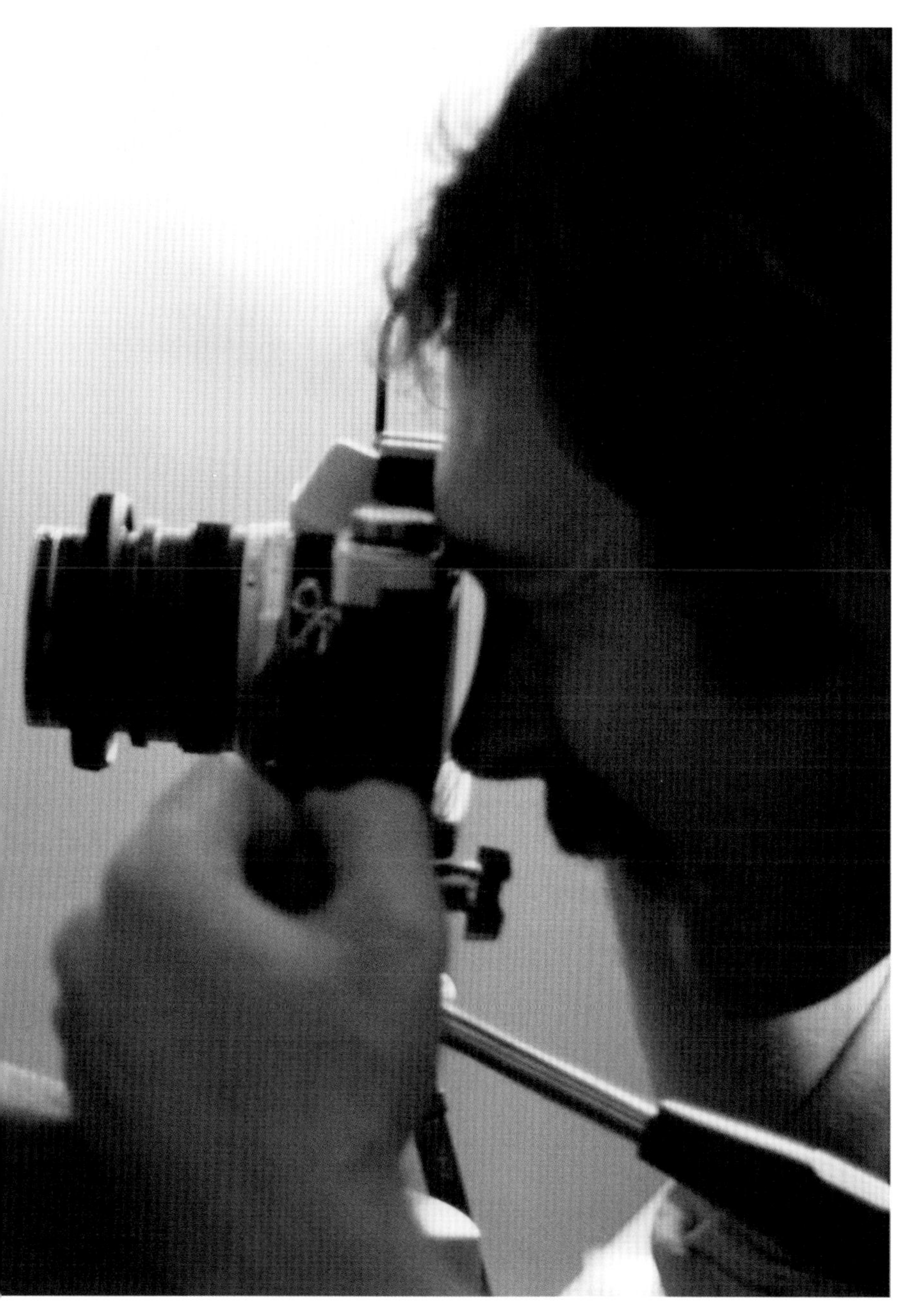

Gerry and Wayne, Montreal c.1975, from the series Friends and Lovers: Coming Out in the 1970s, Montreal

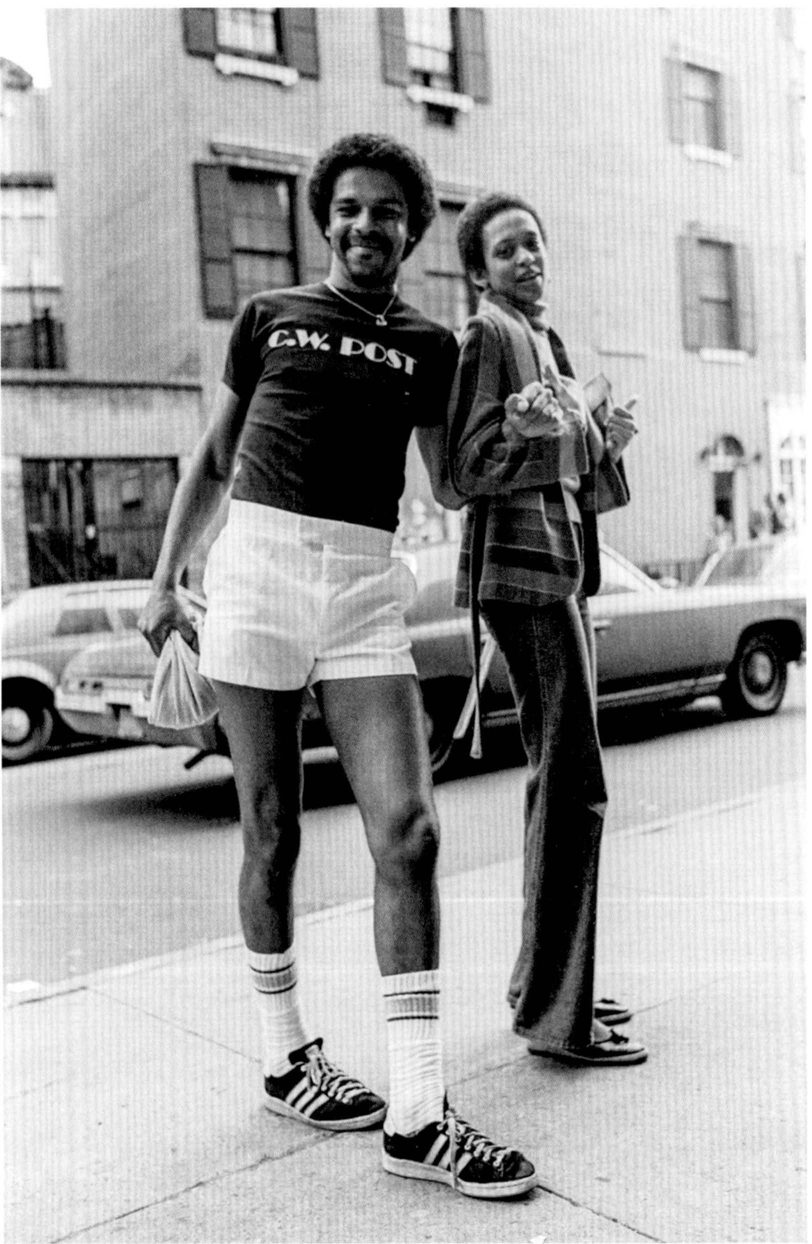

 Above and opposite: *Christopher Street, New York* 1976

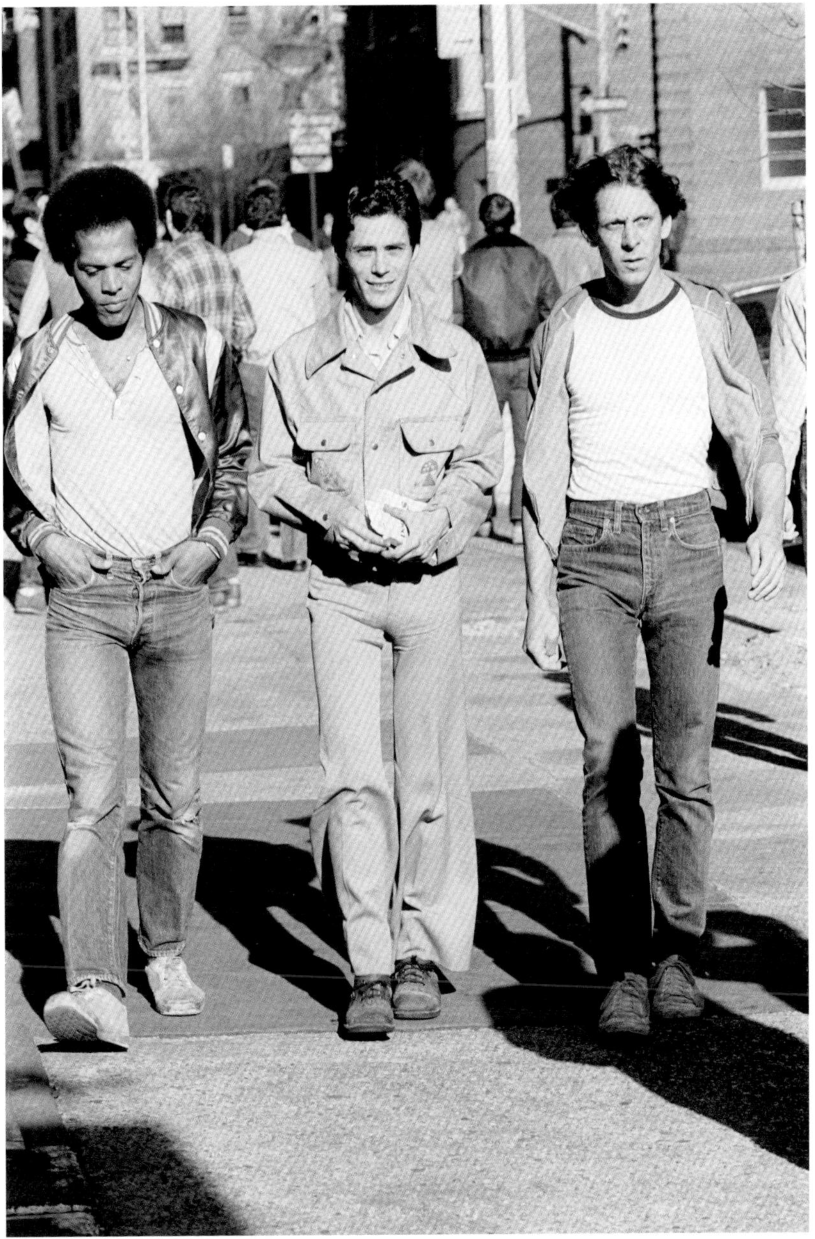

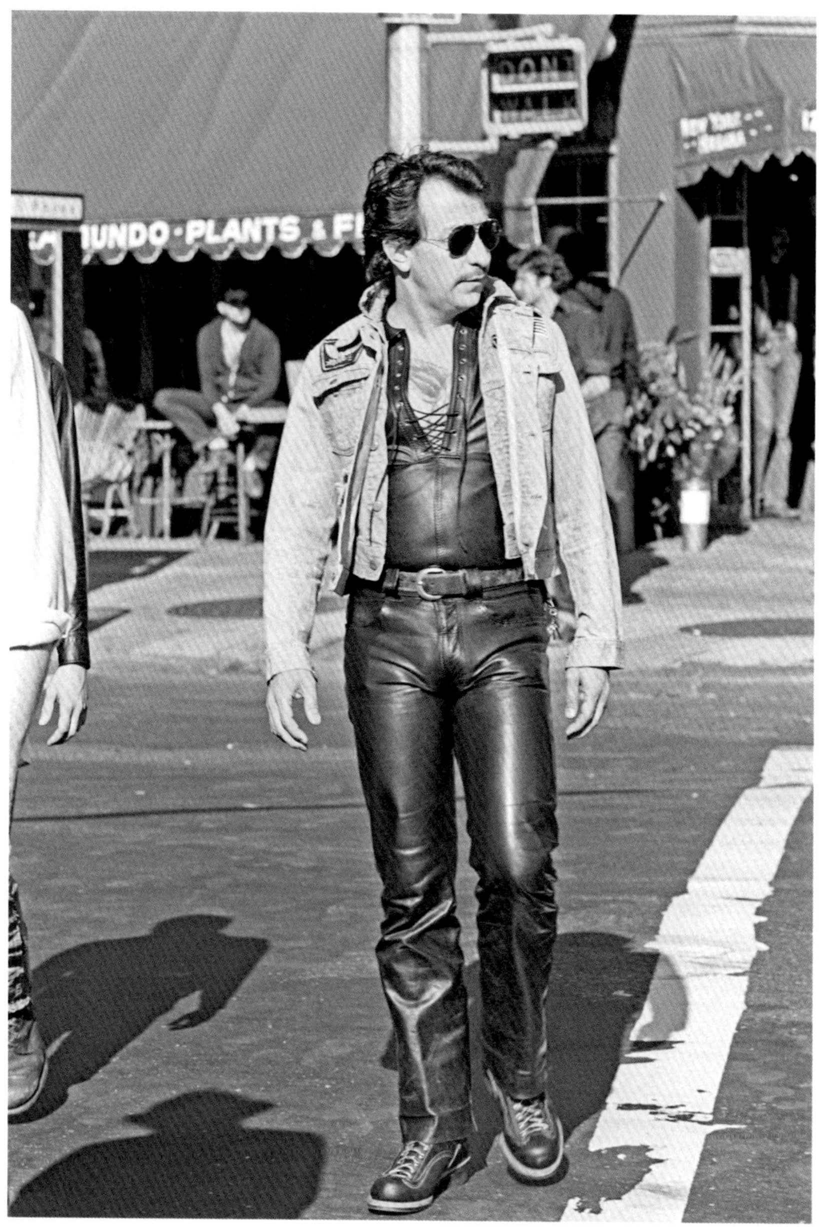

Above and opposite: *Christopher Street, New York* 1976

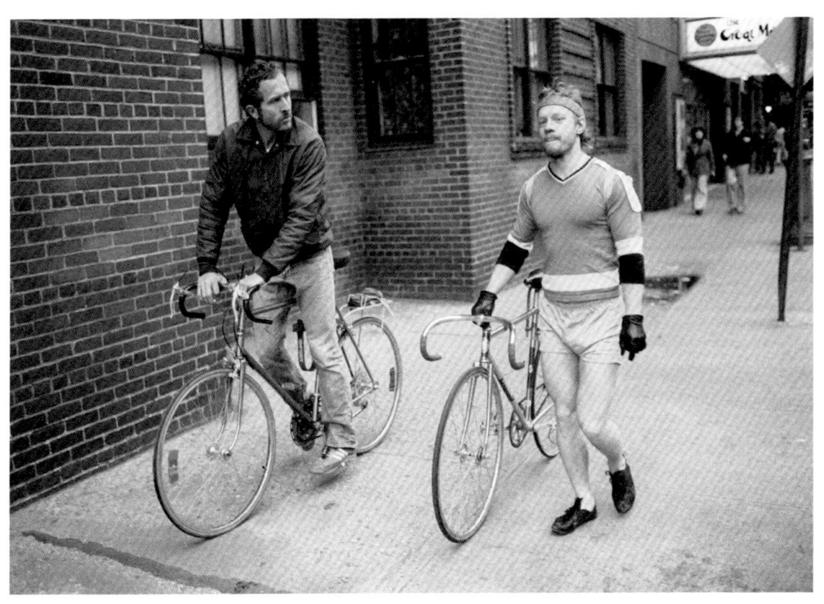

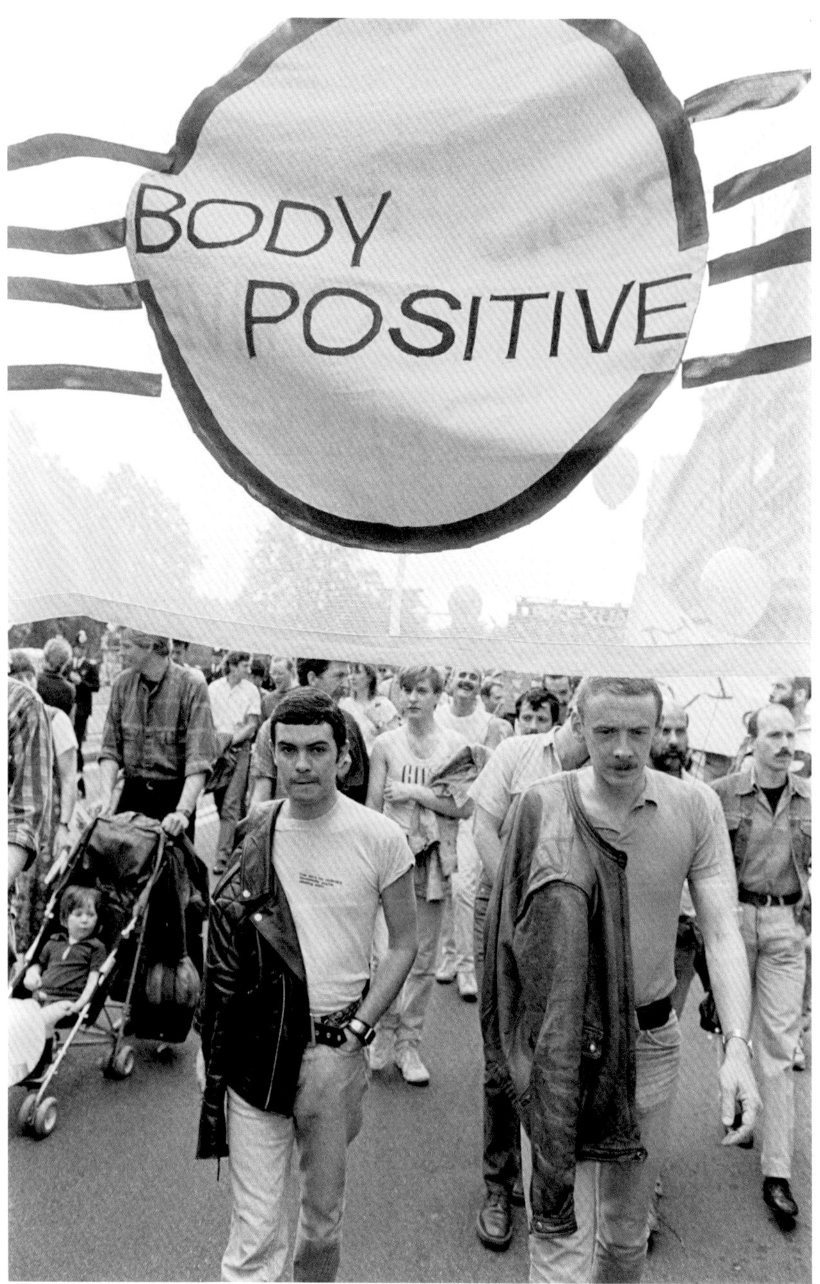

Untitled #8 1985, from the series Come Out, London

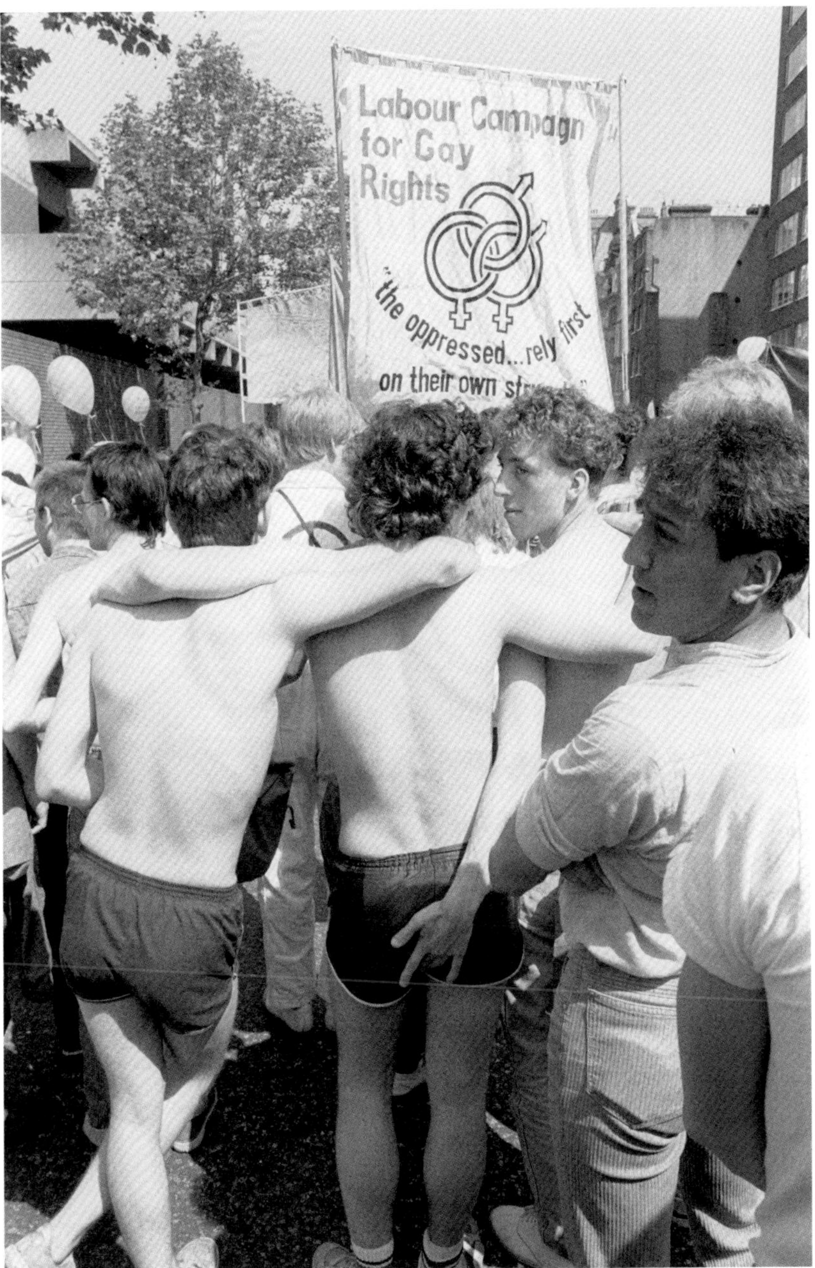

Untitled #3 1984, from the series Come Out, London

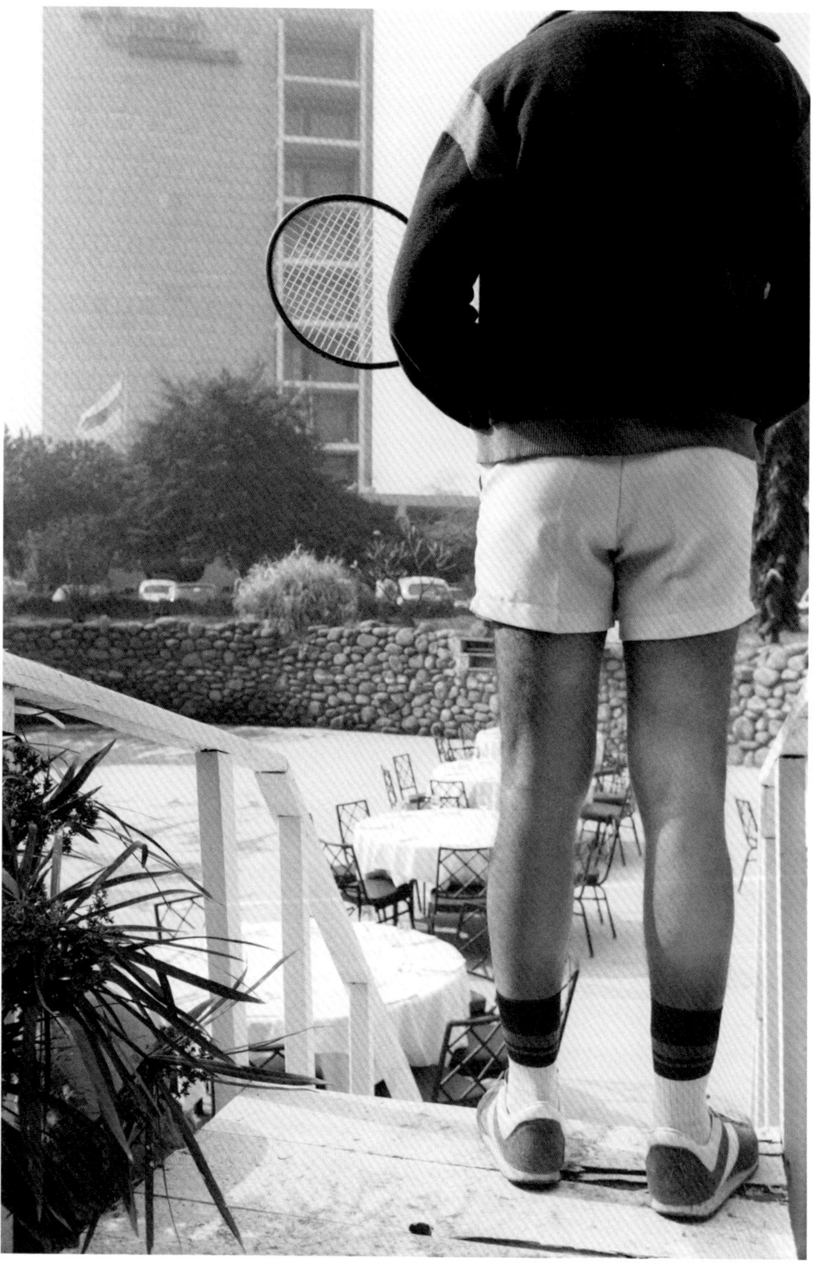

Oberoi Hotel c.1982, from the series Towards an Indian Gay Image

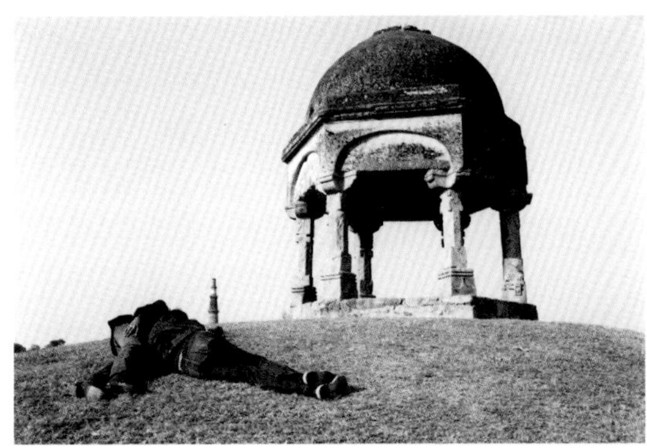

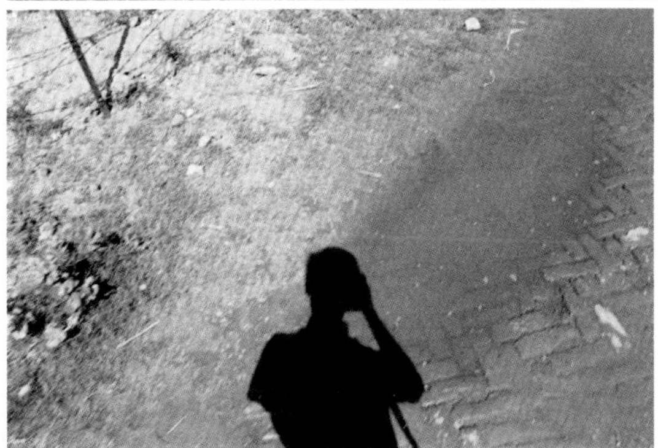

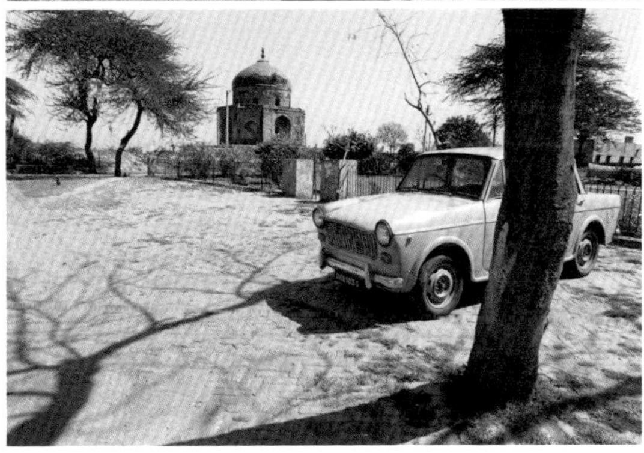

Top: *Qutb Minar* c.1982, from the series Towards an Indian Gay Image
Middle and bottom: from the series Cruising Delhi in the 1980s, c.1983

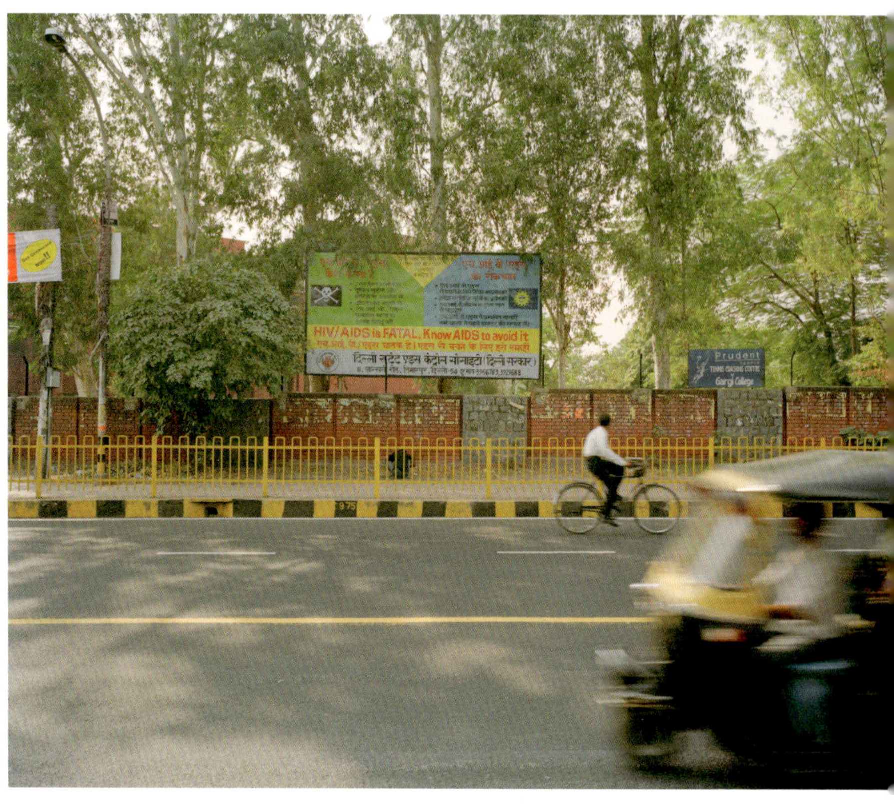

AIDS poster, New Delhi/AIDS protest, Washington DC 2023, from the series Homelands

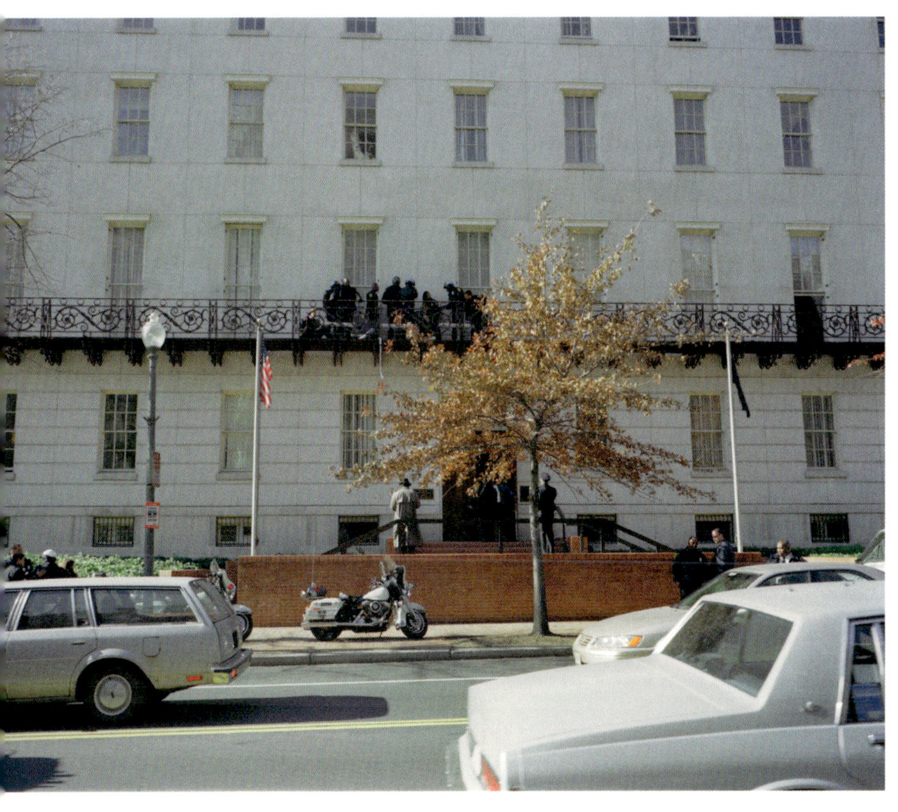

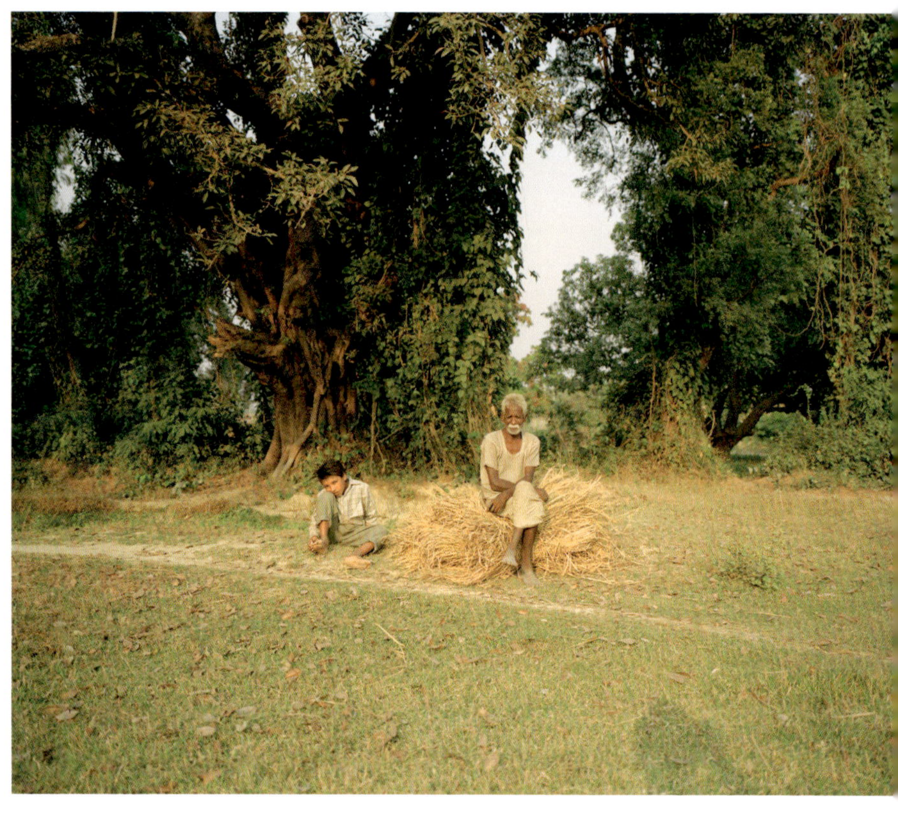

Mundia Pamar, Uttar Pradesh / Bar Harbour, Maine 2023, from the series Homelands

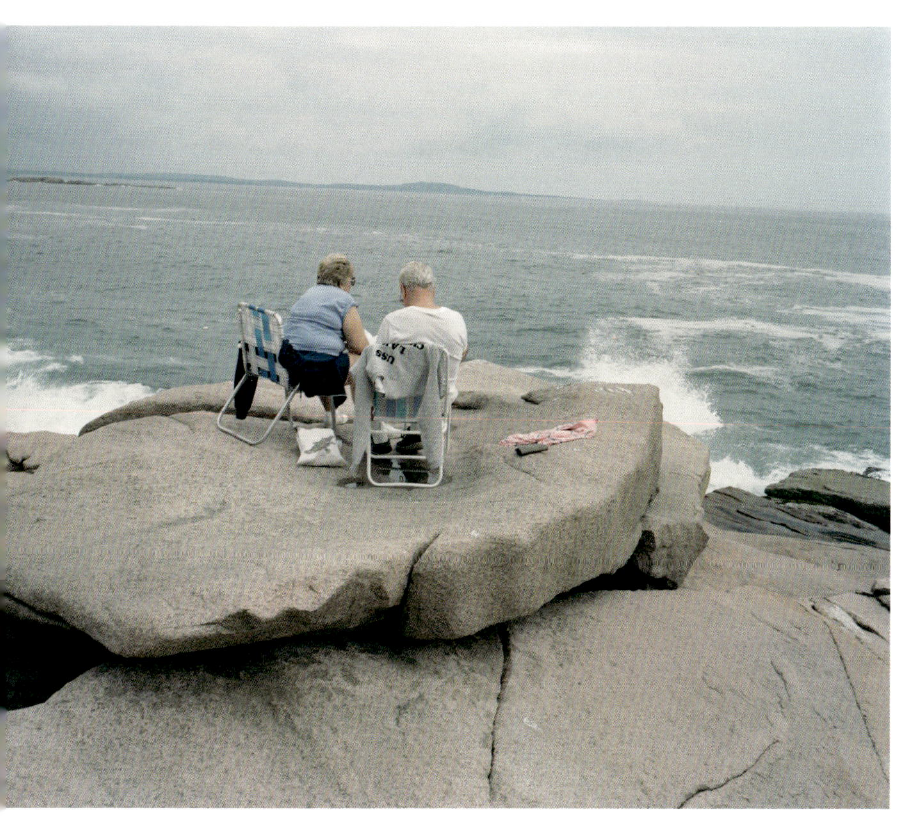

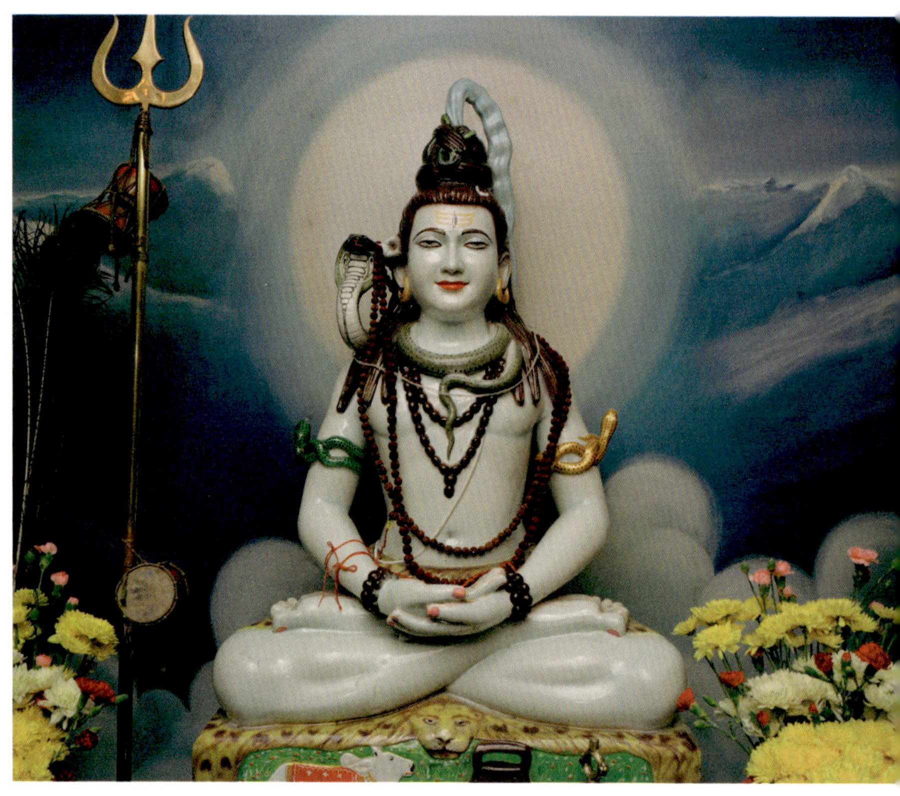

Queens, New York / Embankment, London, from the series Homelands

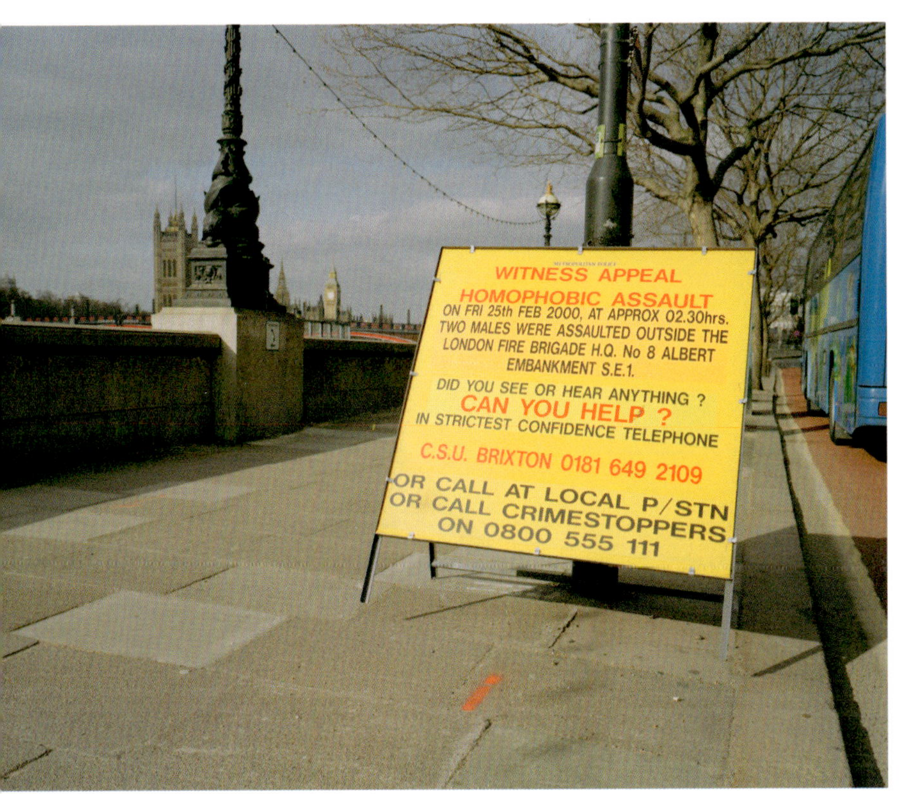
WITNESS APPEAL
HOMOPHOBIC ASSAULT
ON FRI 25th FEB 2000, AT APPROX 02.30hrs.
TWO MALES WERE ASSAULTED OUTSIDE THE
LONDON FIRE BRIGADE H.Q. No 8 ALBERT
EMBANKMENT S.E.1.
DID YOU SEE OR HEAR ANYTHING ?
CAN YOU HELP ?
IN STRICTEST CONFIDENCE TELEPHONE
C.S.U. BRIXTON 0181 649 2109
OR CALL AT LOCAL P/STN
OR CALL CRIMESTOPPERS
ON 0800 555 111

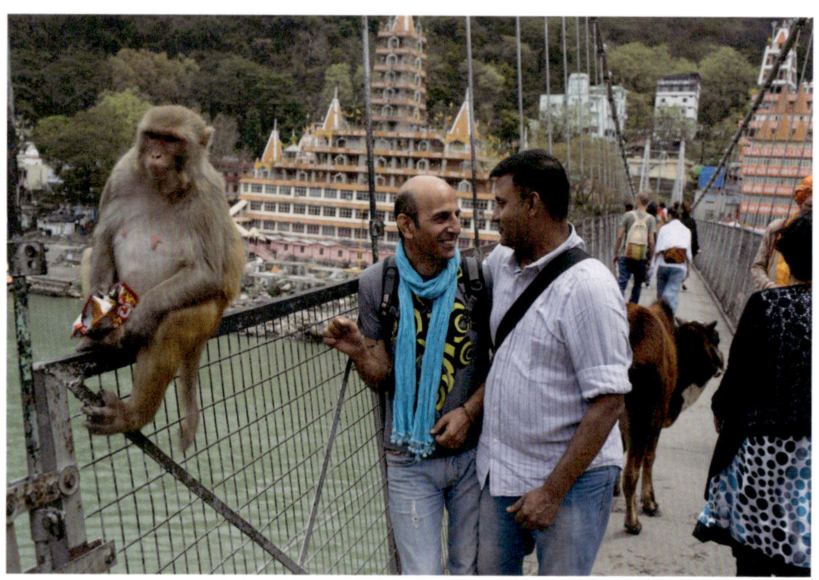

 Ranjan and Zahid 2015, from the series Dissent and Desire, Rishikesh

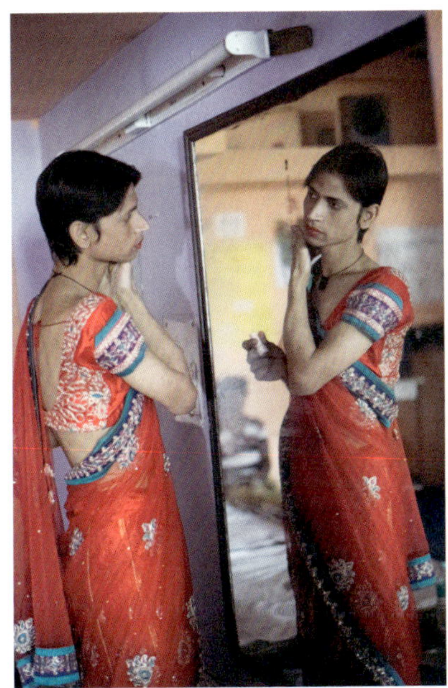

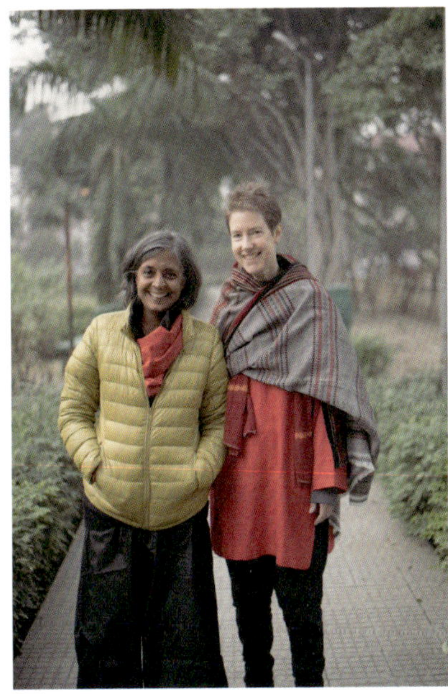

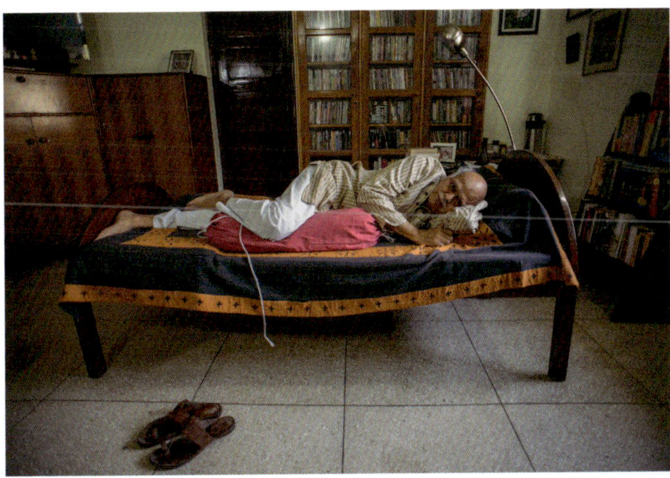

From the series Dissent and Desire
Top: *Rizwan, Delhi* 2015 (left); *Geeta and Kath, Delhi* 2015 (right)
Bottom: *Saleem, Lucknow* 2015

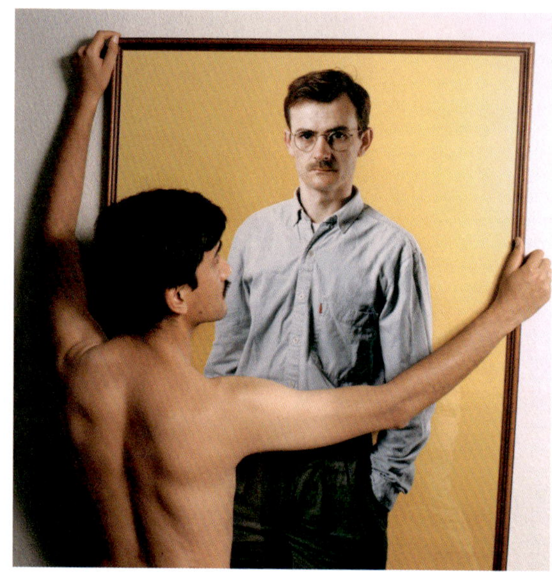

He needed
dope
to get it

up but once
it was
there he was

hooked
on it

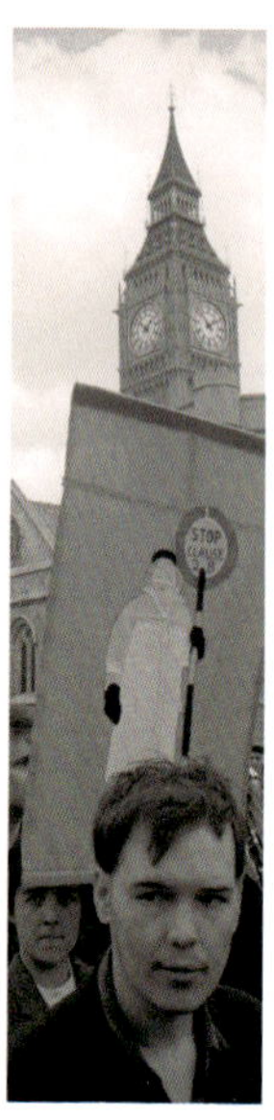

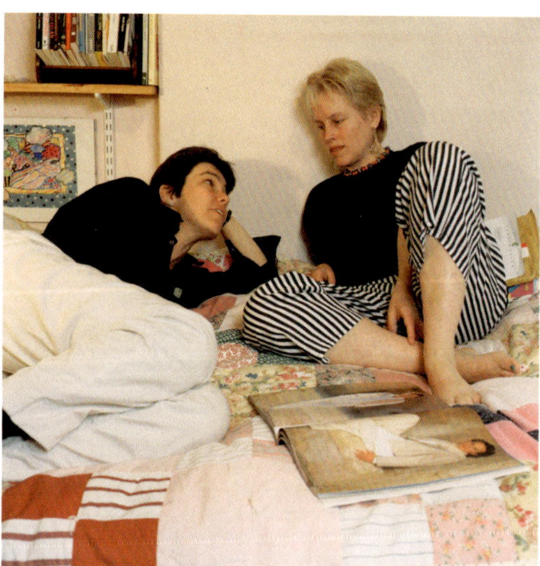

Repeated,
these night time
confessions
over tea
a train

rumbles through
on the pause
of our thought

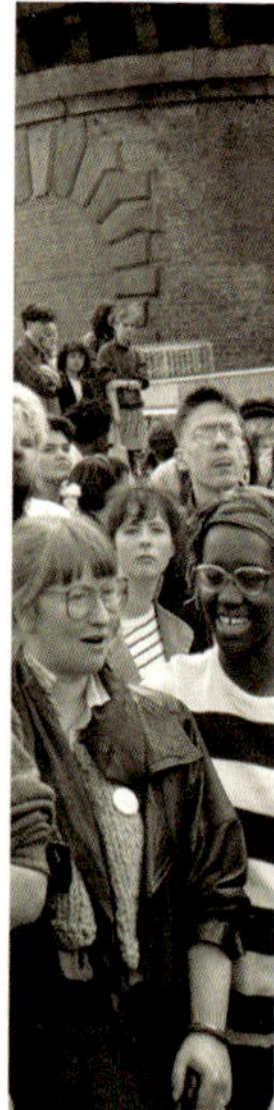

Above and opposite: from the series 'Pretended' Family Relationships, London, 1988

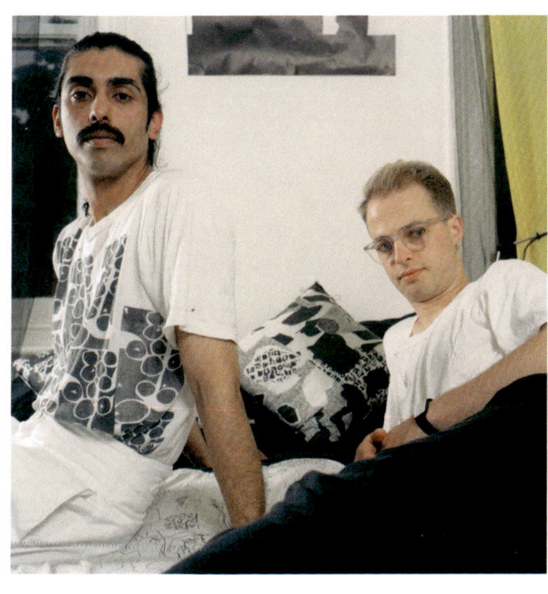

Seeing you, seeing me, it all becomes

so clear

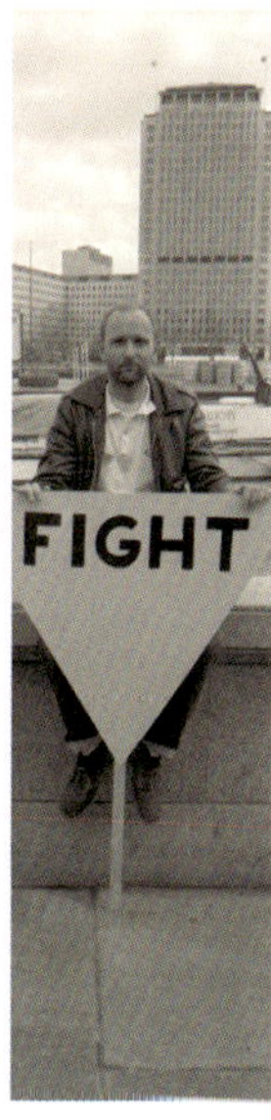

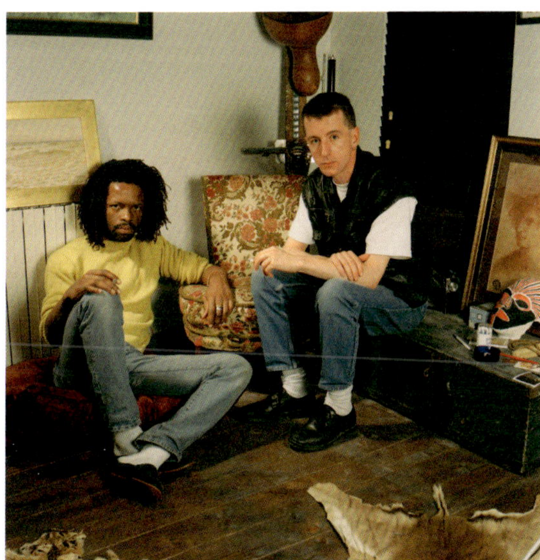

If anger
is a sign of love,
our signs have

locked like scorpions

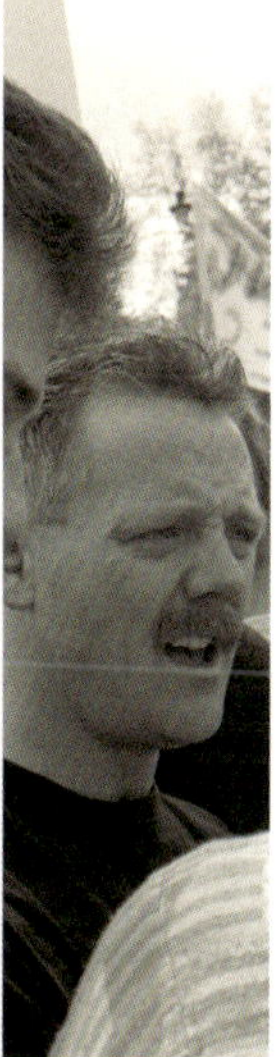

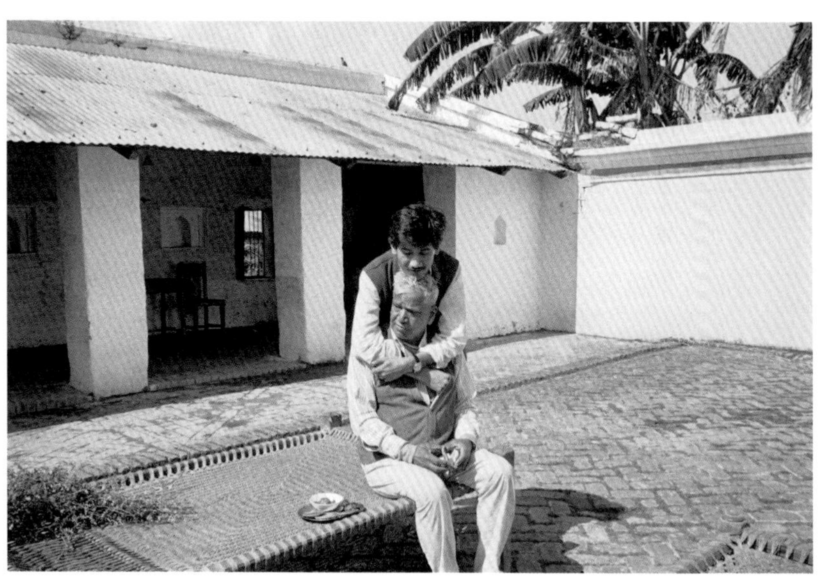

Sunil and his father, Shri Ram, in their ancestral home, Munda Pamar, Uttar Pradesh c.1982, from the series Country: Portrait of an Indian Village

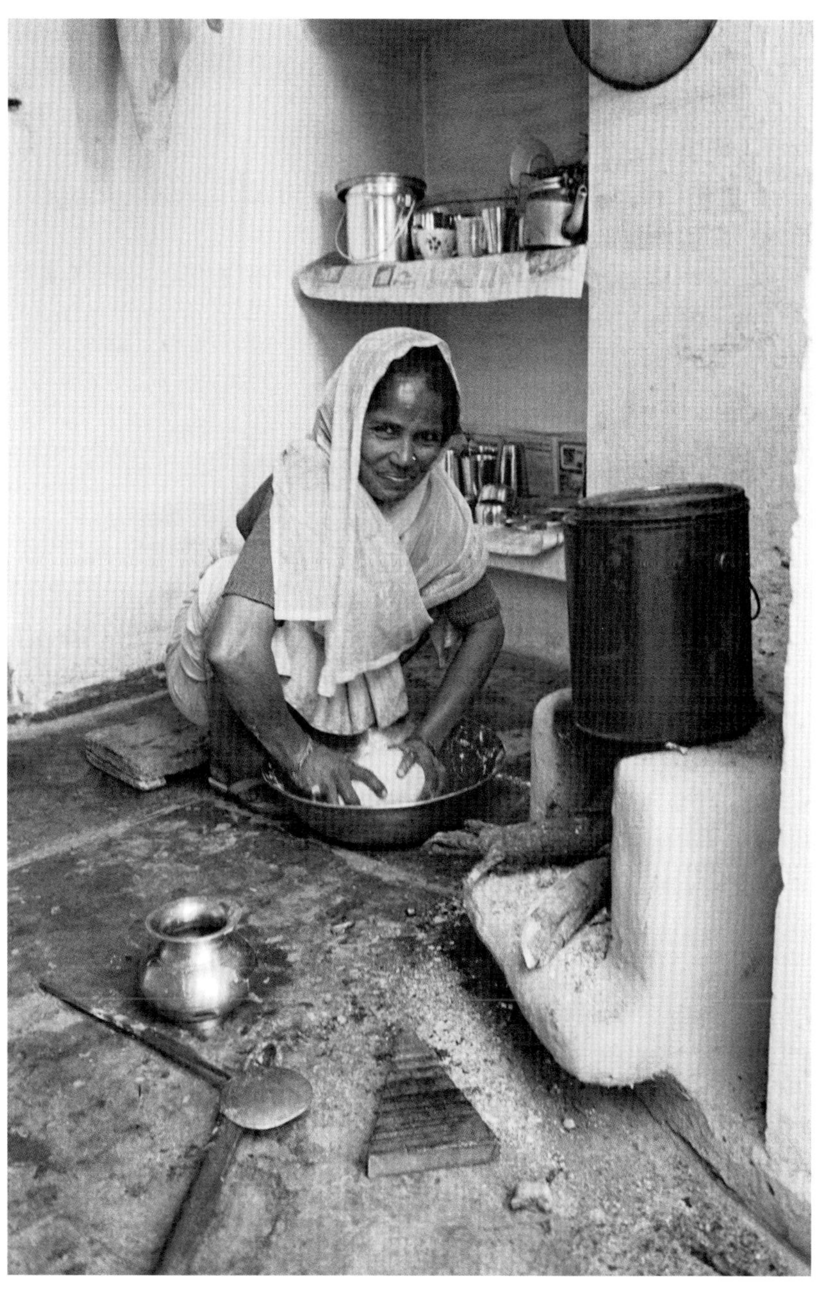

Aunt Uttam, teacher, Munda Pamar, Uttar Pradesh c.1982, from the series Country: Portrait of an Indian Village

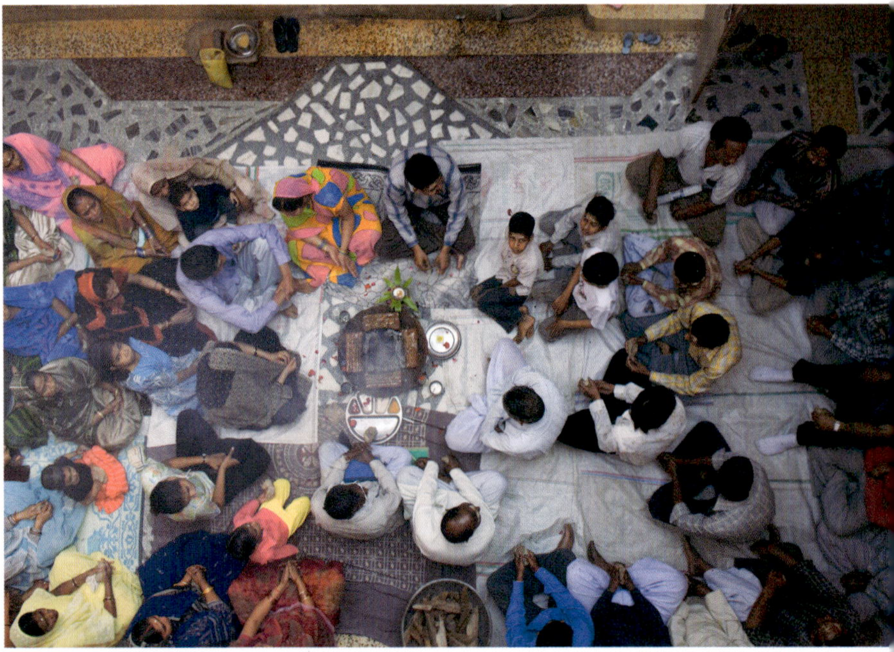

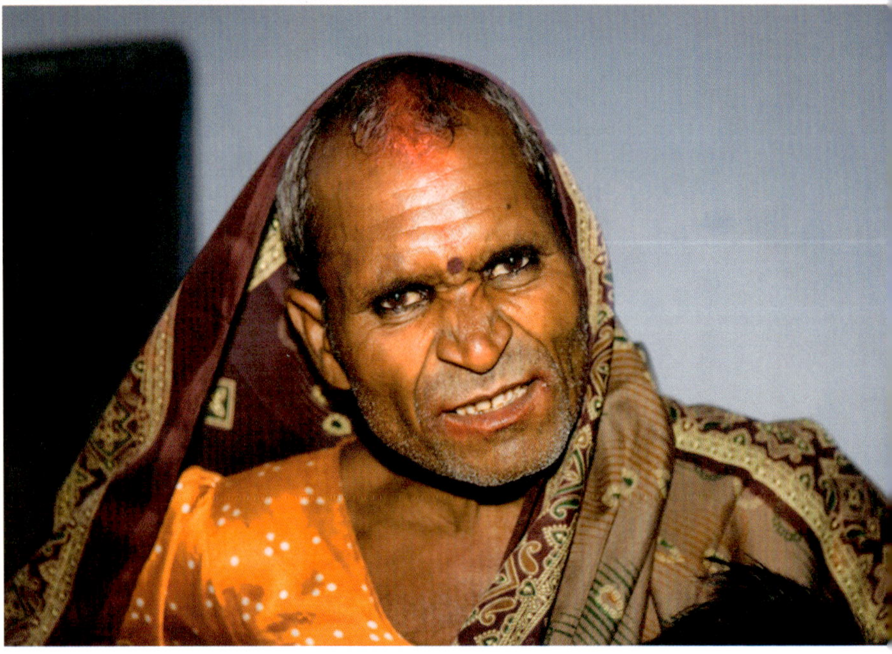

From the series Country: Portrait of an Indian Village c.2005. Top: *Havan/House*
Bottom: *Holi/Freedom Fighters, Munda Pamar, Uttar Pradesh*

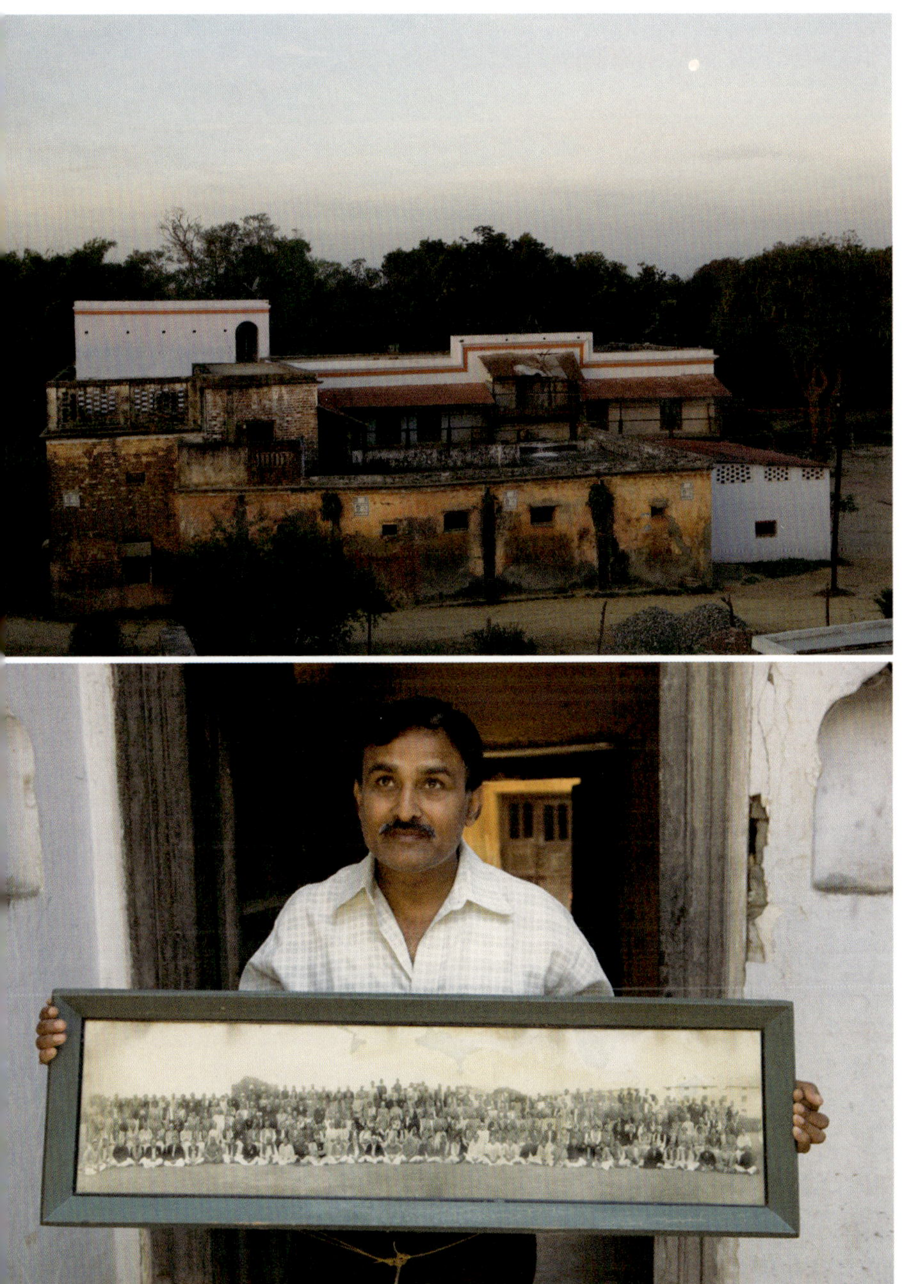

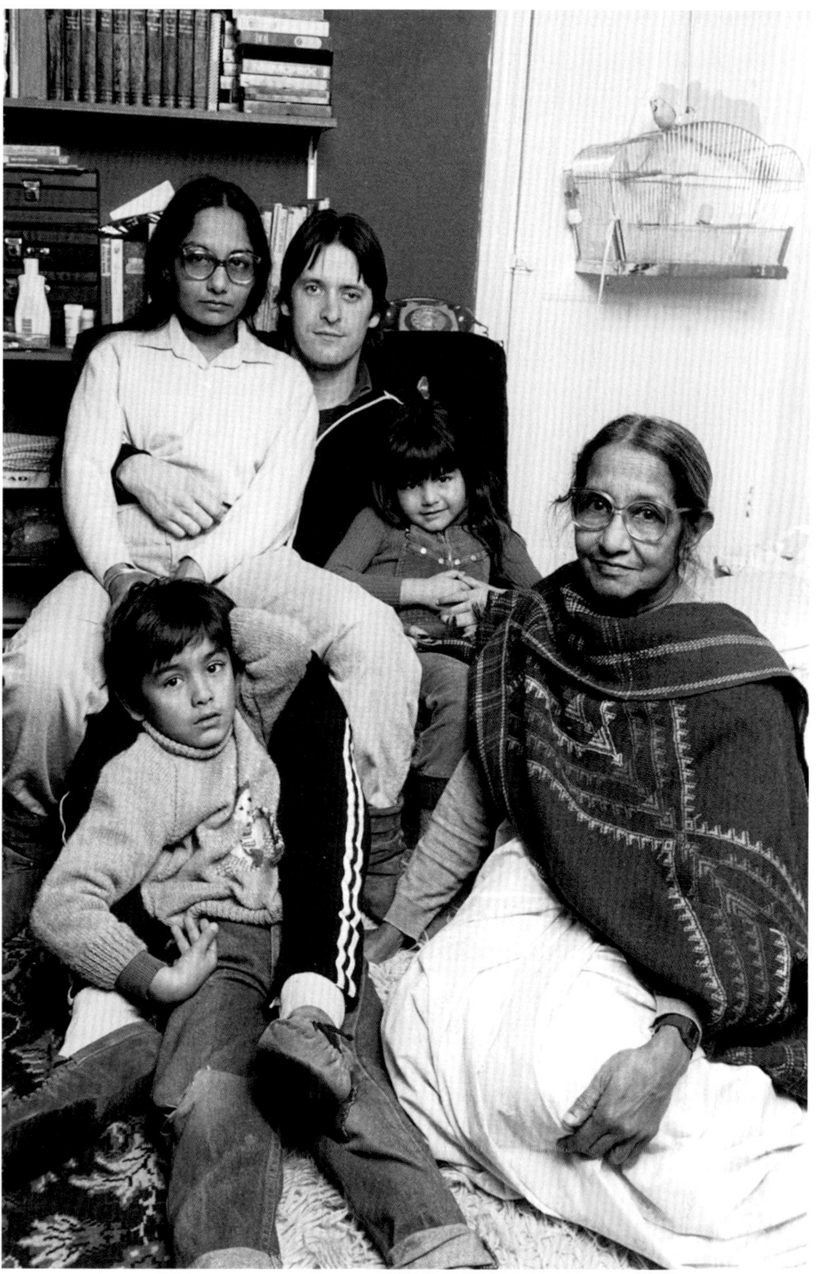

Family 1986, from the series Black Experience, London

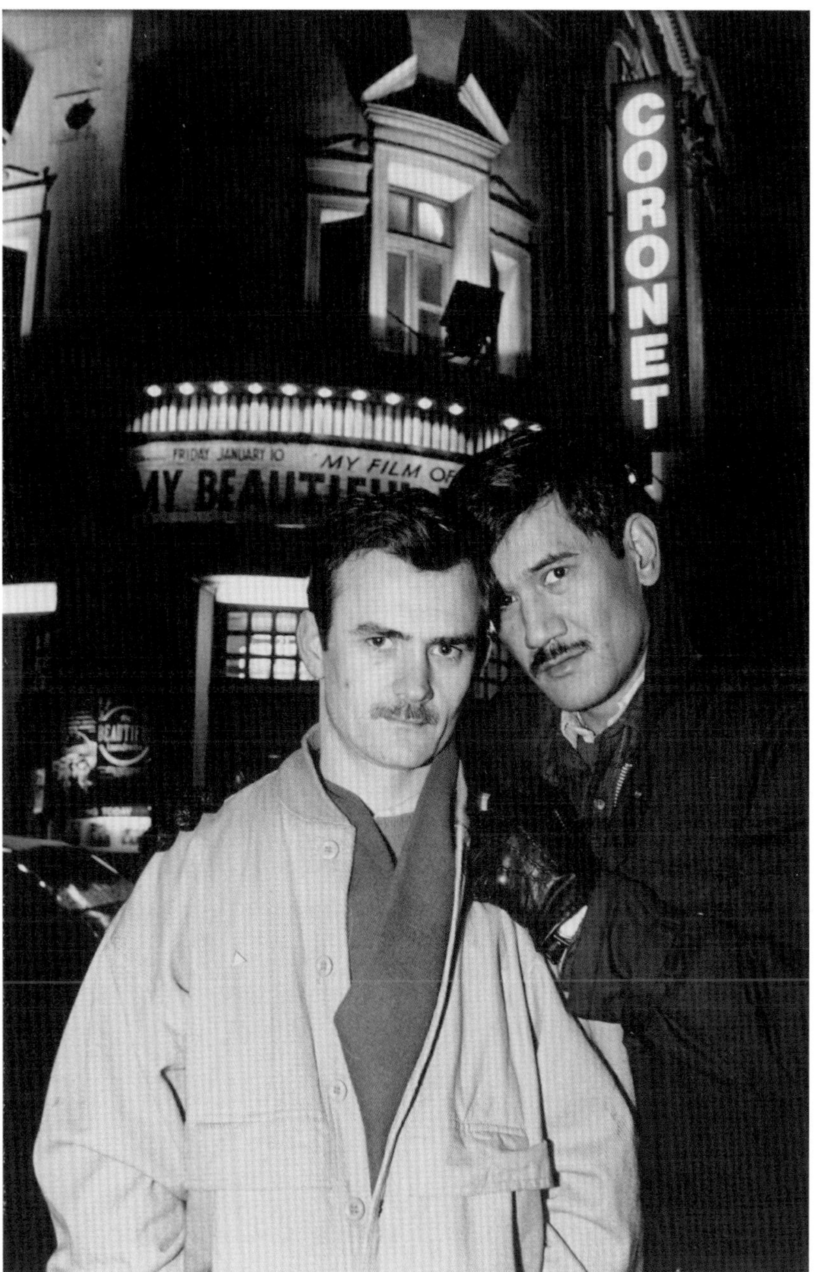

 Gay 1986, from the series Black Experience, London

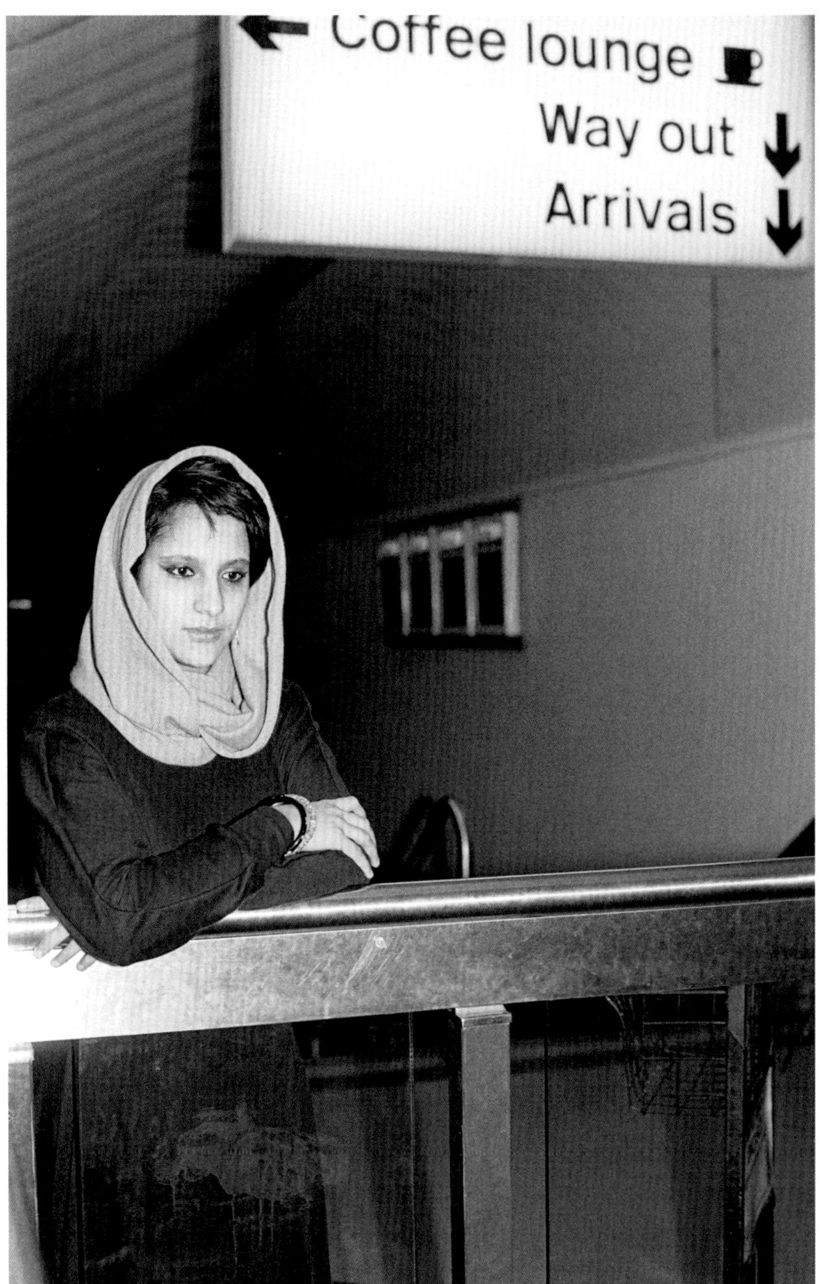

Migrant 1986, from the series Black Experience, London

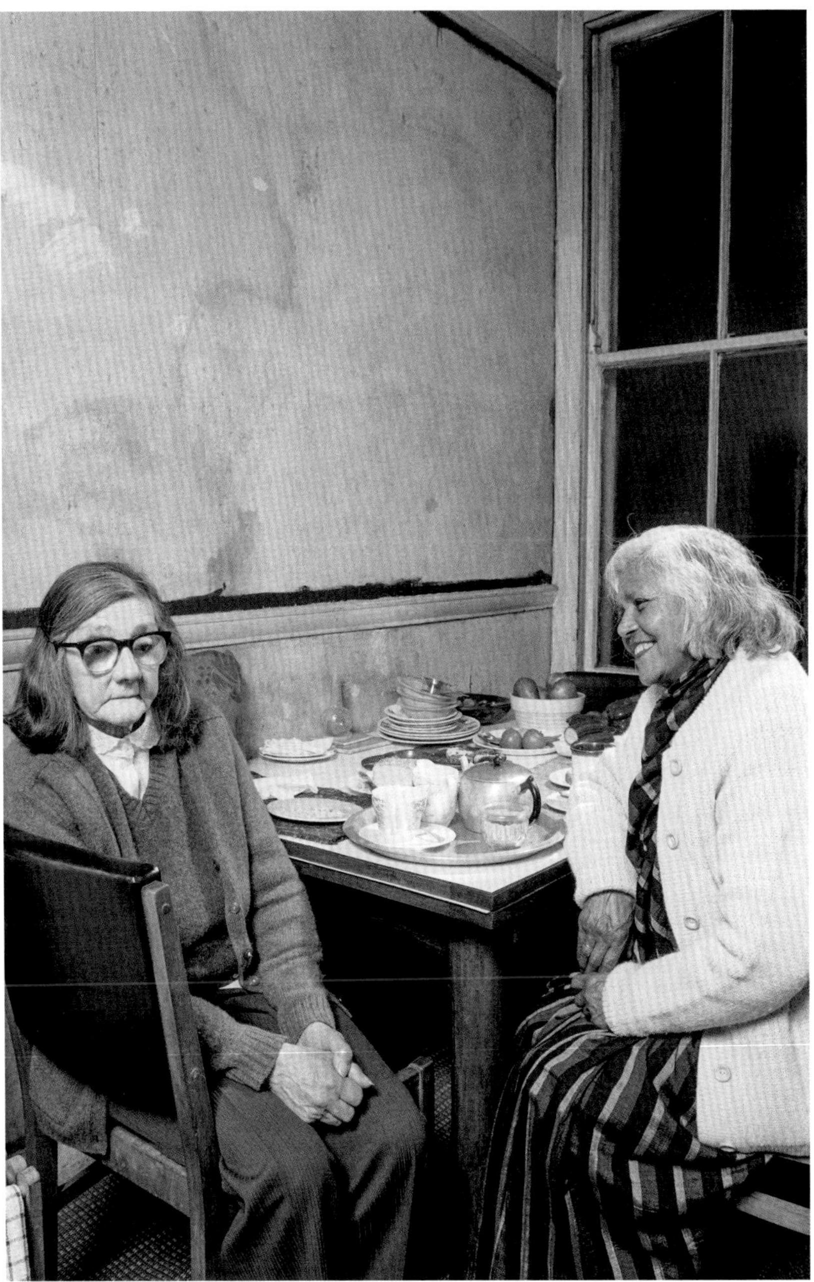

Elderly 1986, from the series Black Experience, London

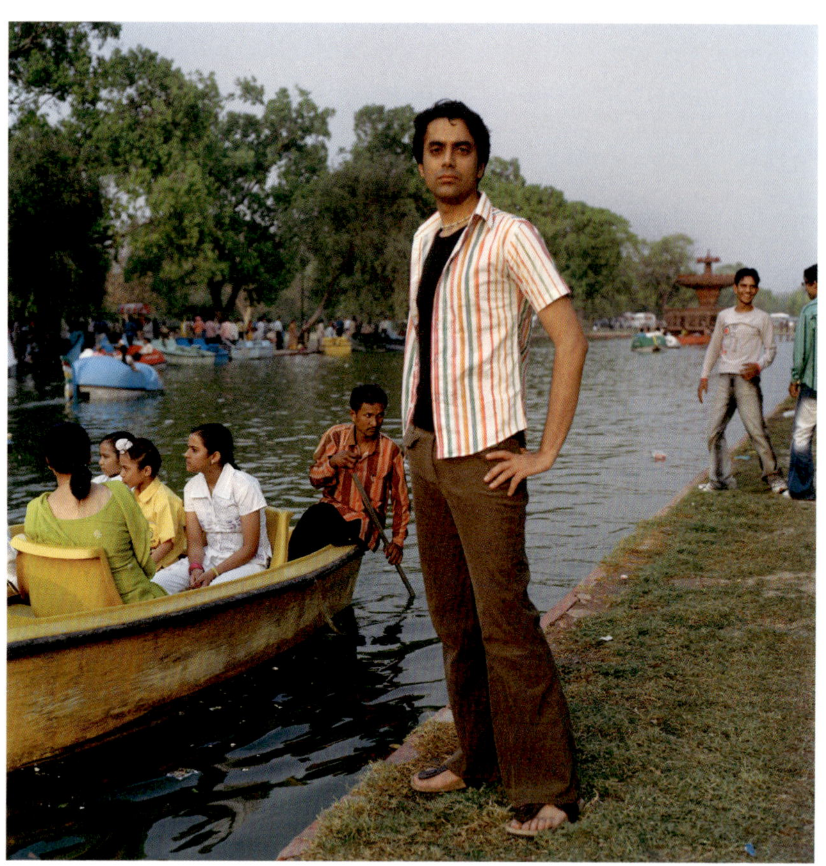

 Bikram 2007, from the series Mr Malhotra's Party, Delhi

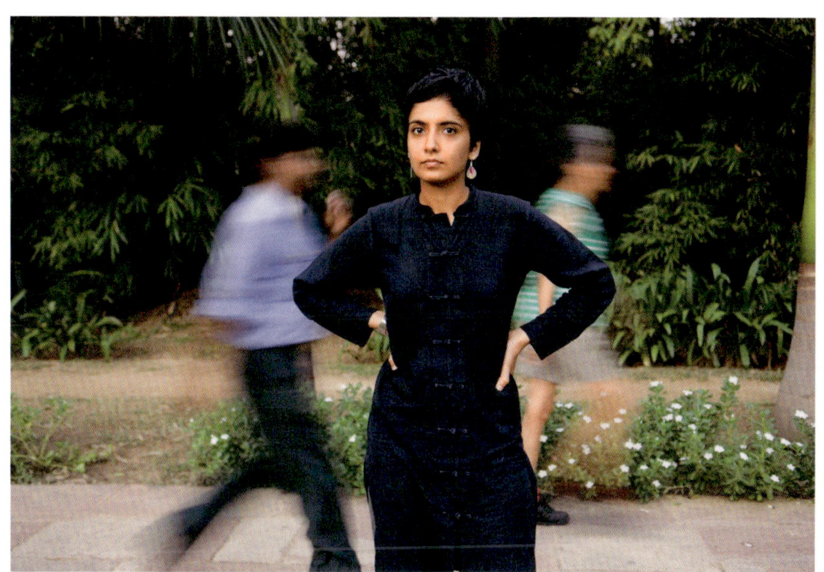

Anokhi 2004, from the series Mr Malhotra's Party, Delhi

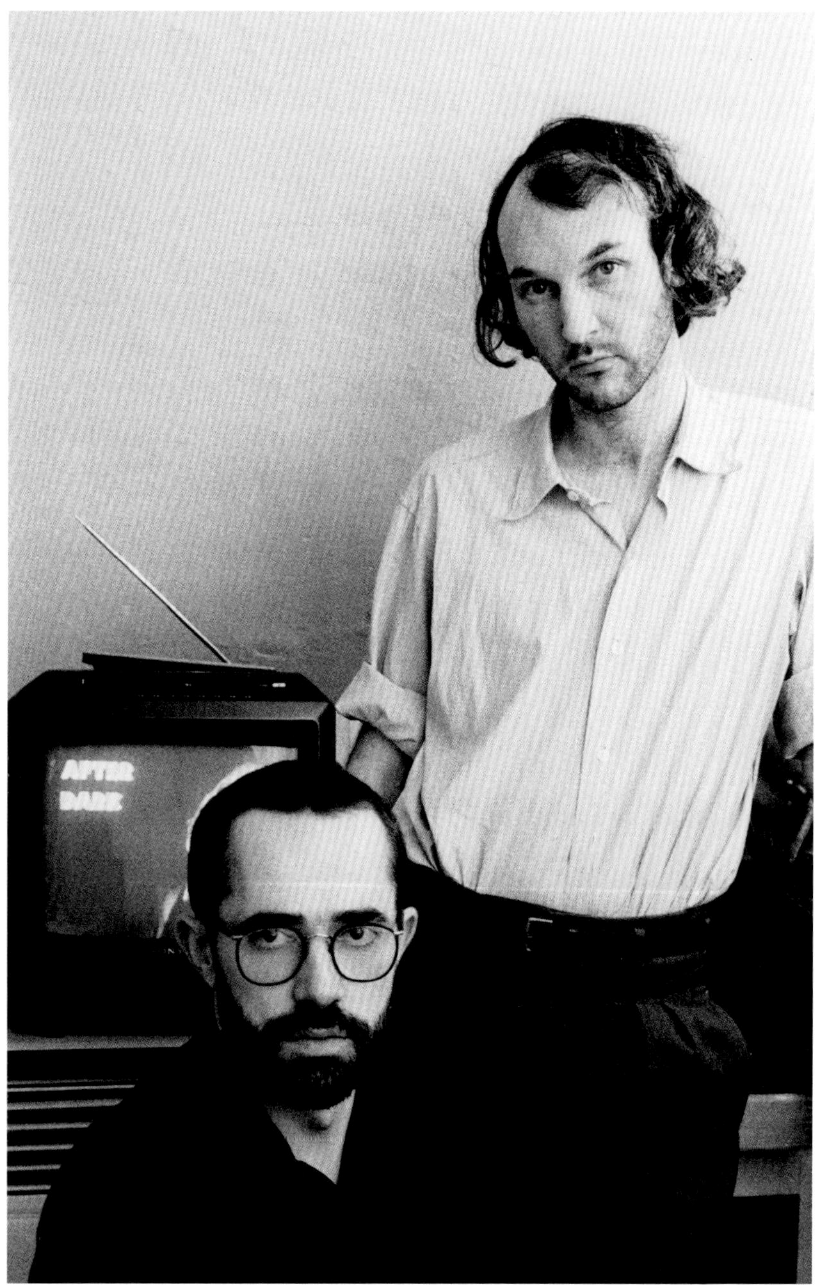

Guy and Brian 1984, from the series Lovers: Ten Years On, London

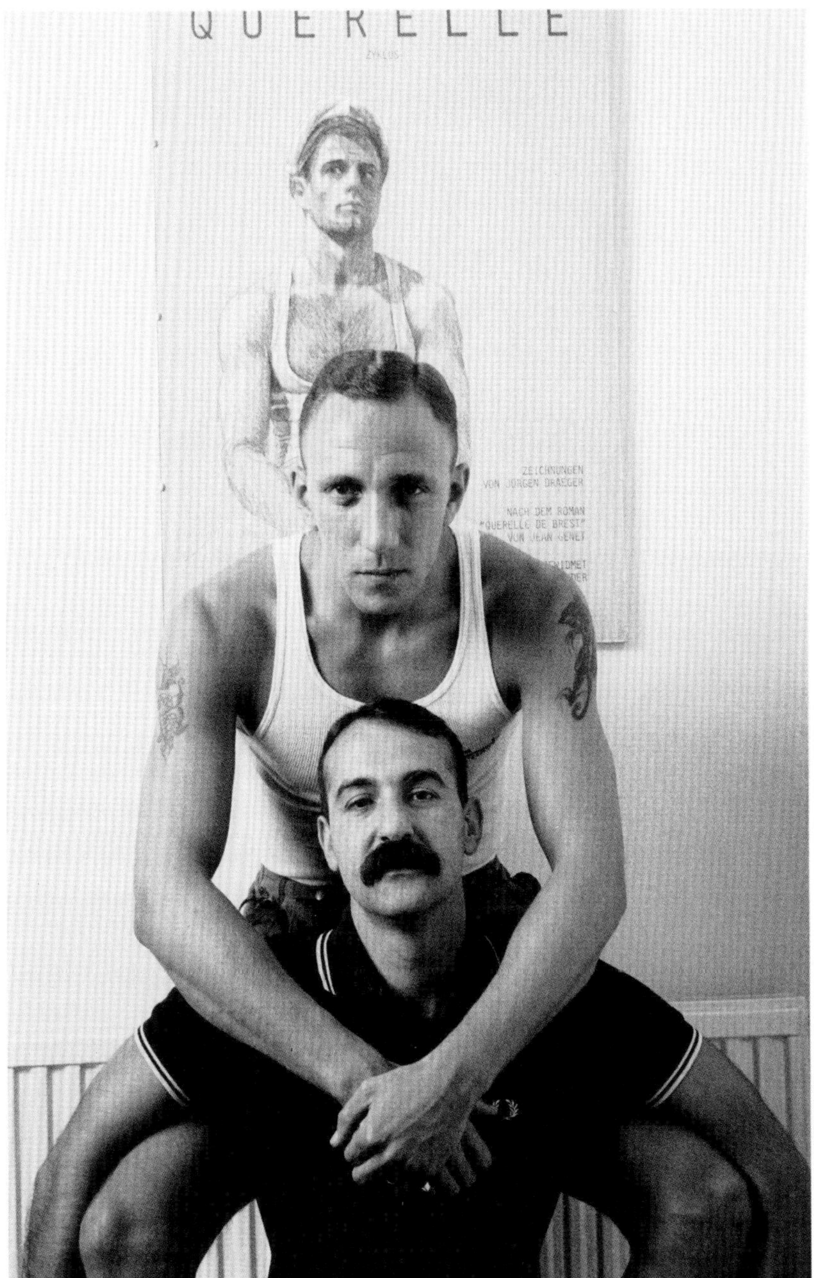

Ian and Pavlik 1984, from the series Lovers: Ten Years On, London

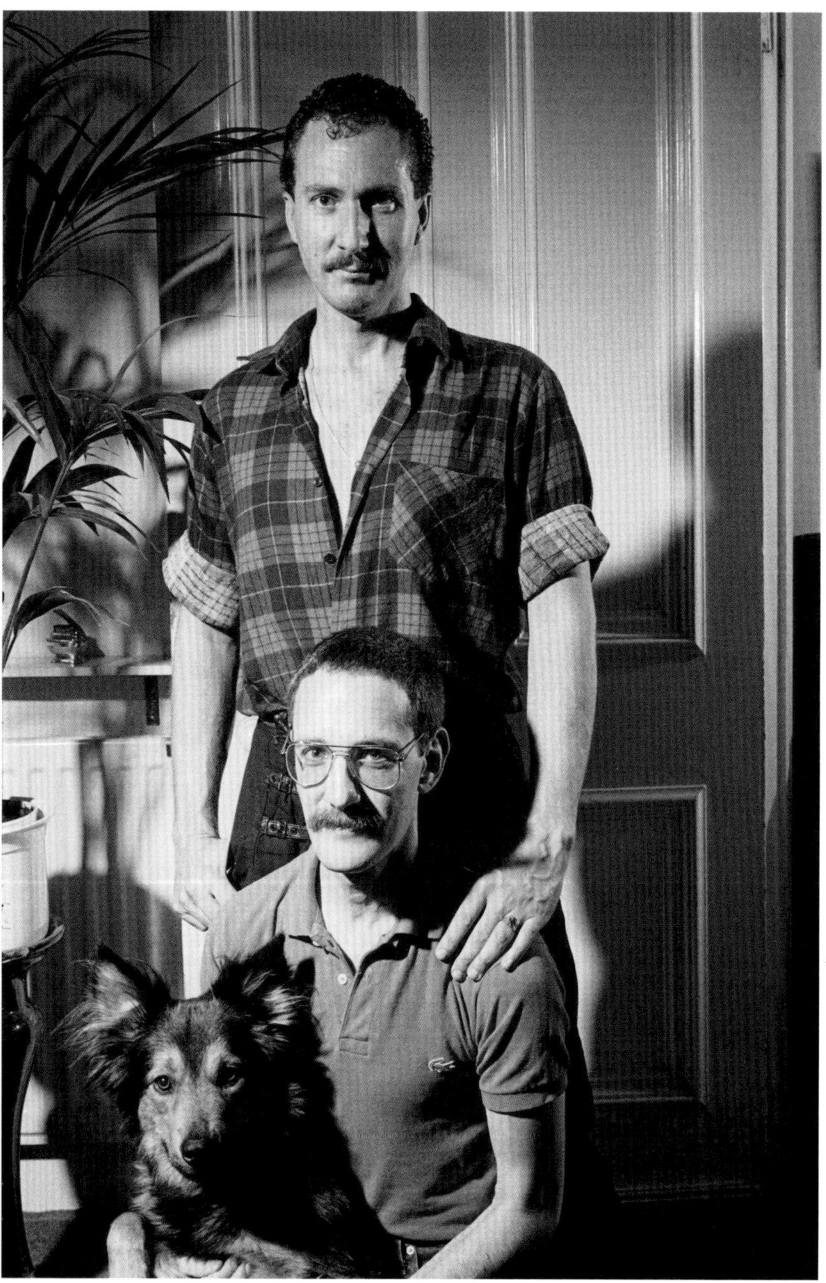

Pablo and Charlie 1985, from the series Lovers: Ten Years On, London

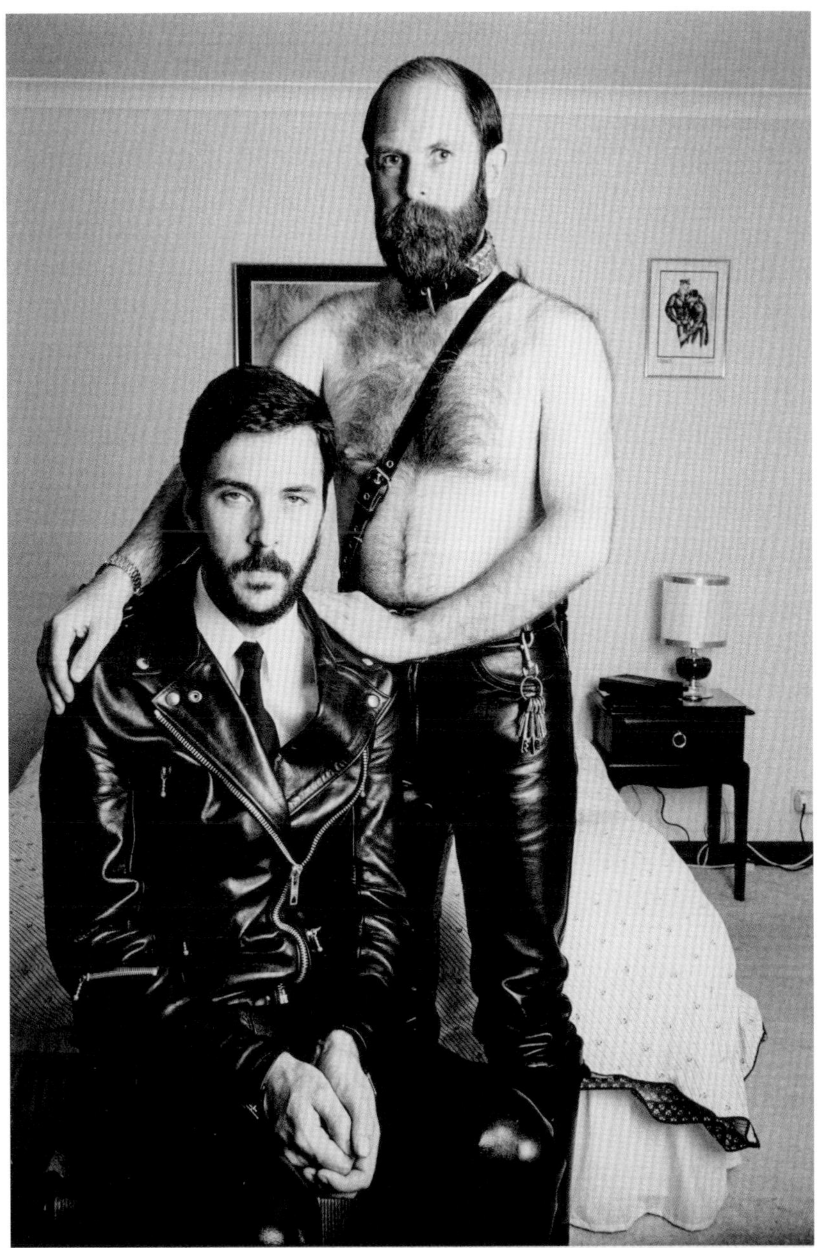

 Dylan and Gerald 1985, from the series Lovers: Ten Years On, London

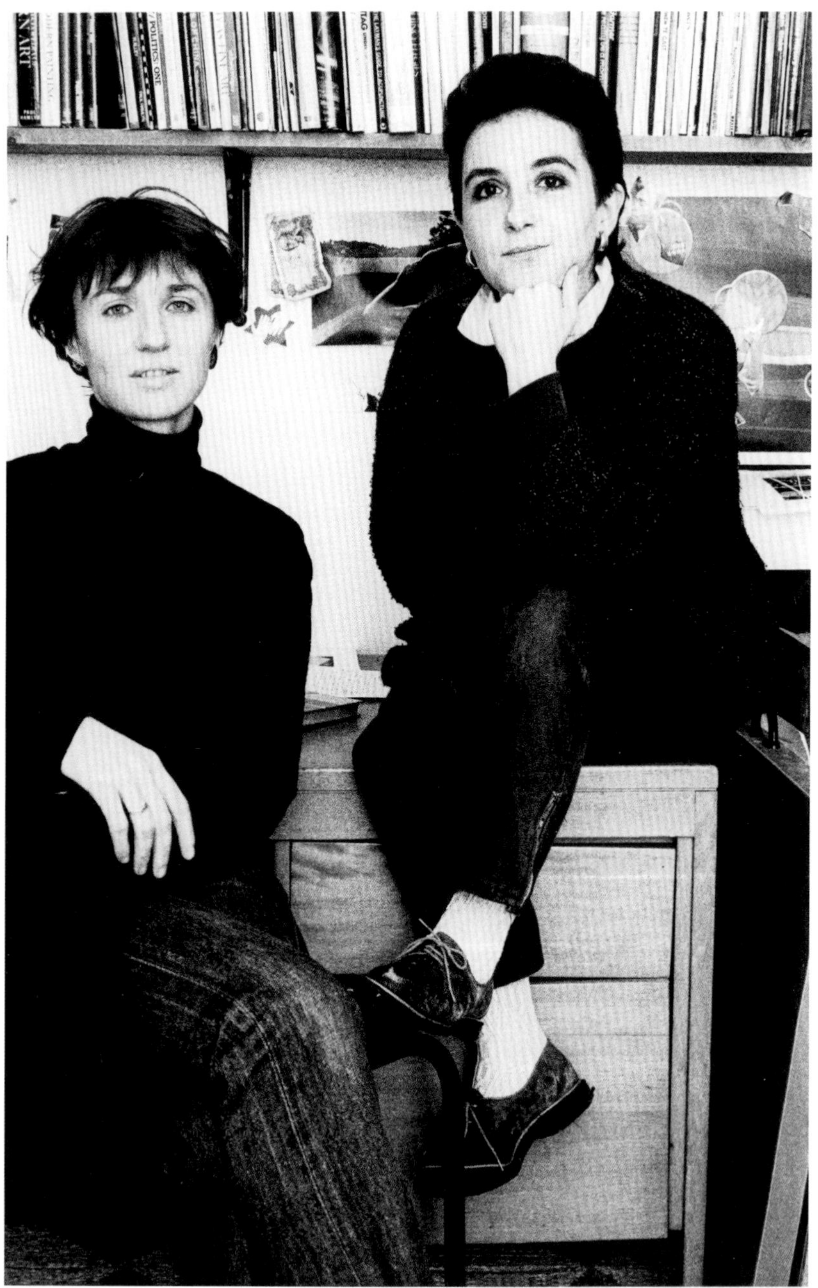

Sue and Yve 1984, from the series Lovers: Ten Years On, London

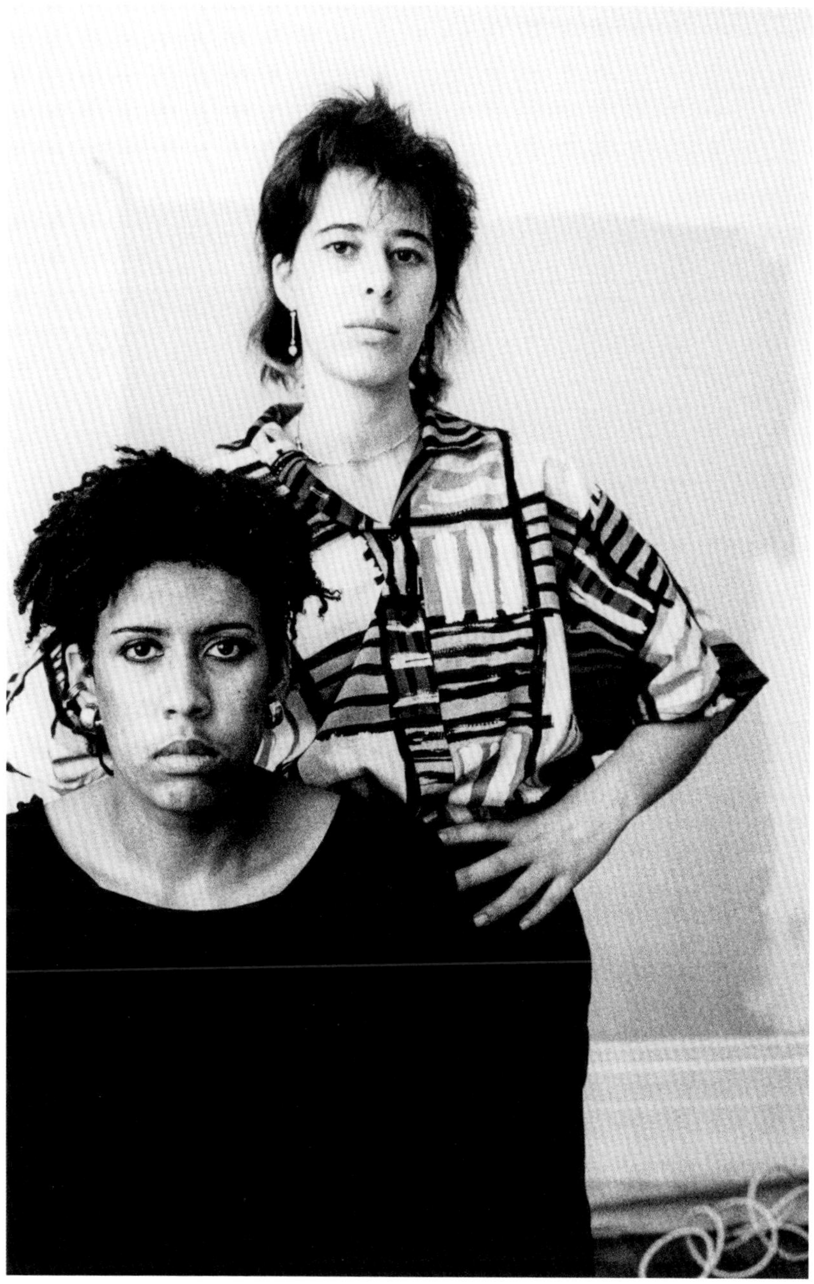

Lisa and Emily 1984, from the series Lovers: Ten Years On, London

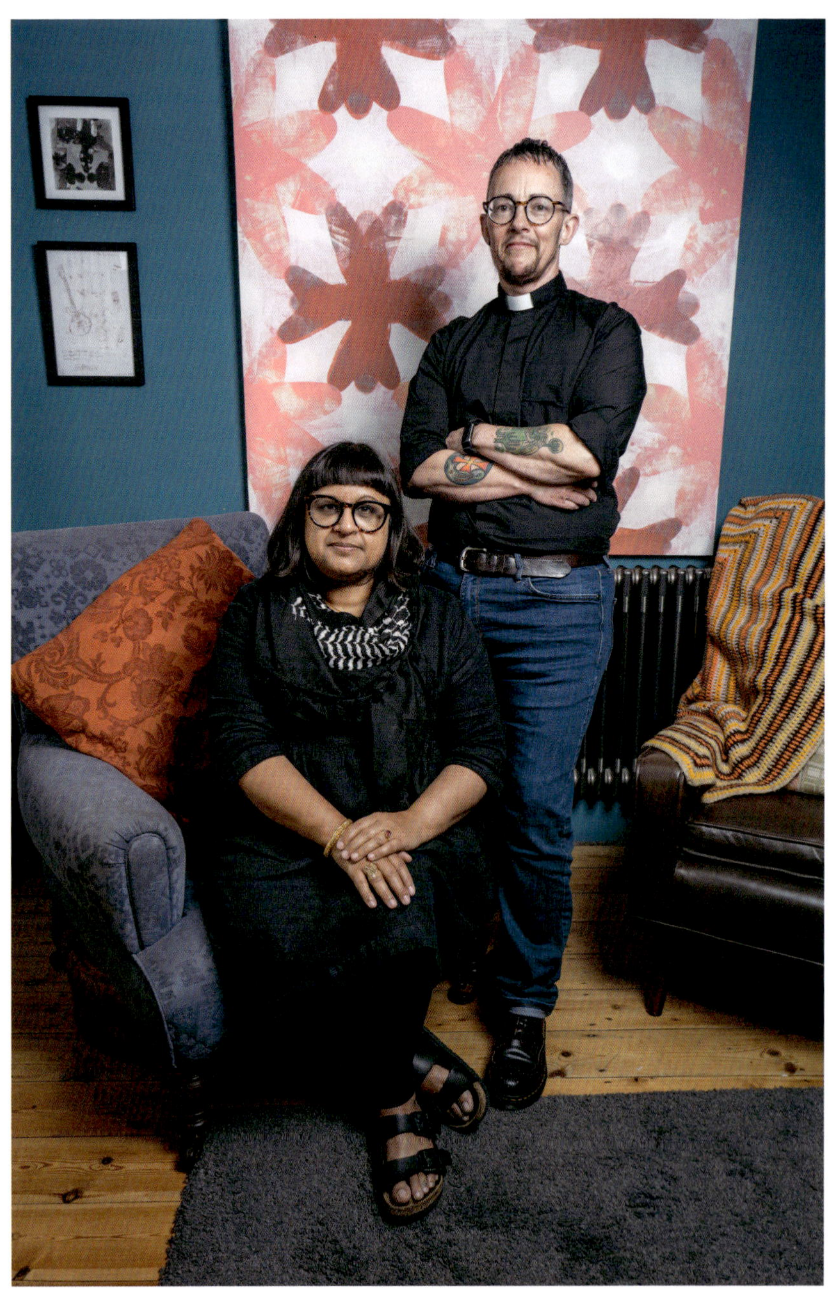

Nazmia and Grey 2024, from the series Lovers Revisited, London (made in collaboration with Charan Singh)

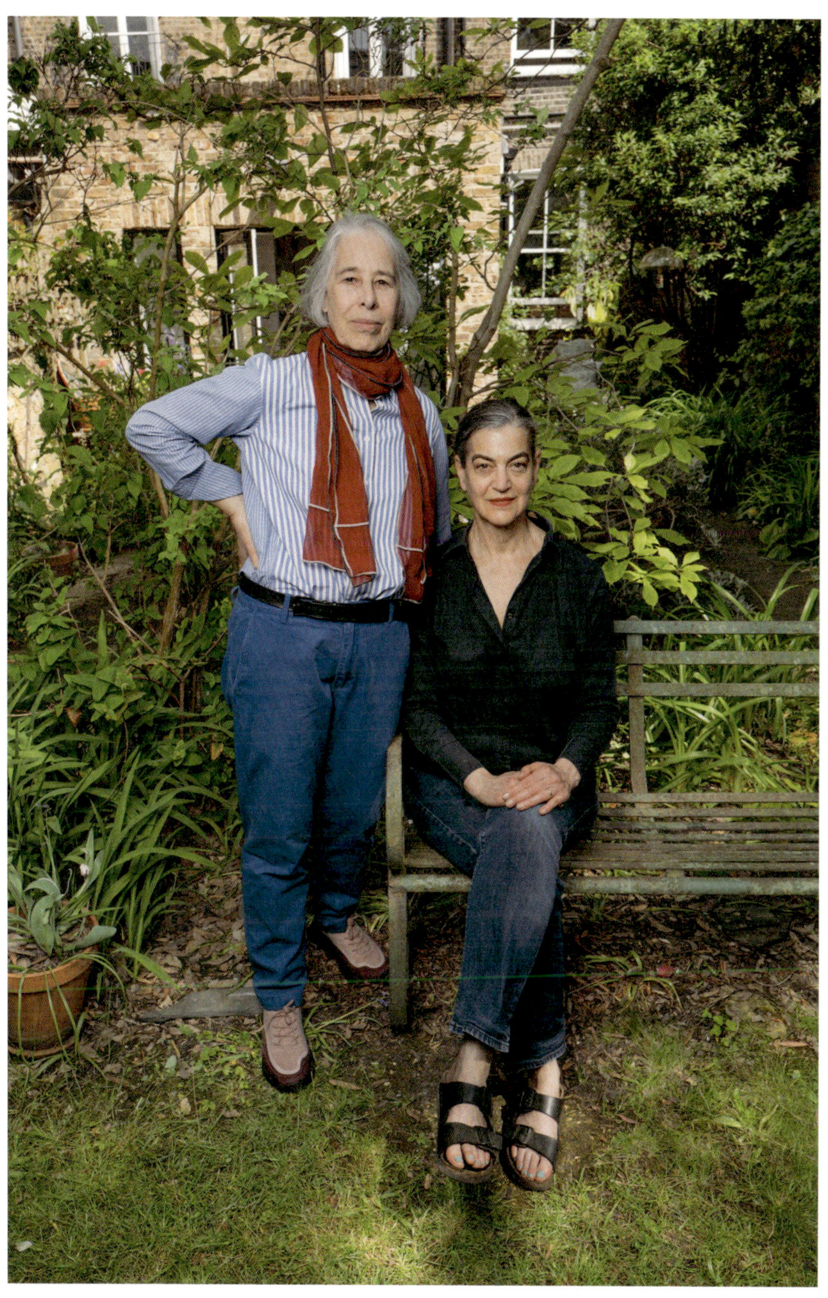

Emily and Renée 2024, from the series Lovers Revisited, London (made in collaboration with Charan Singh)

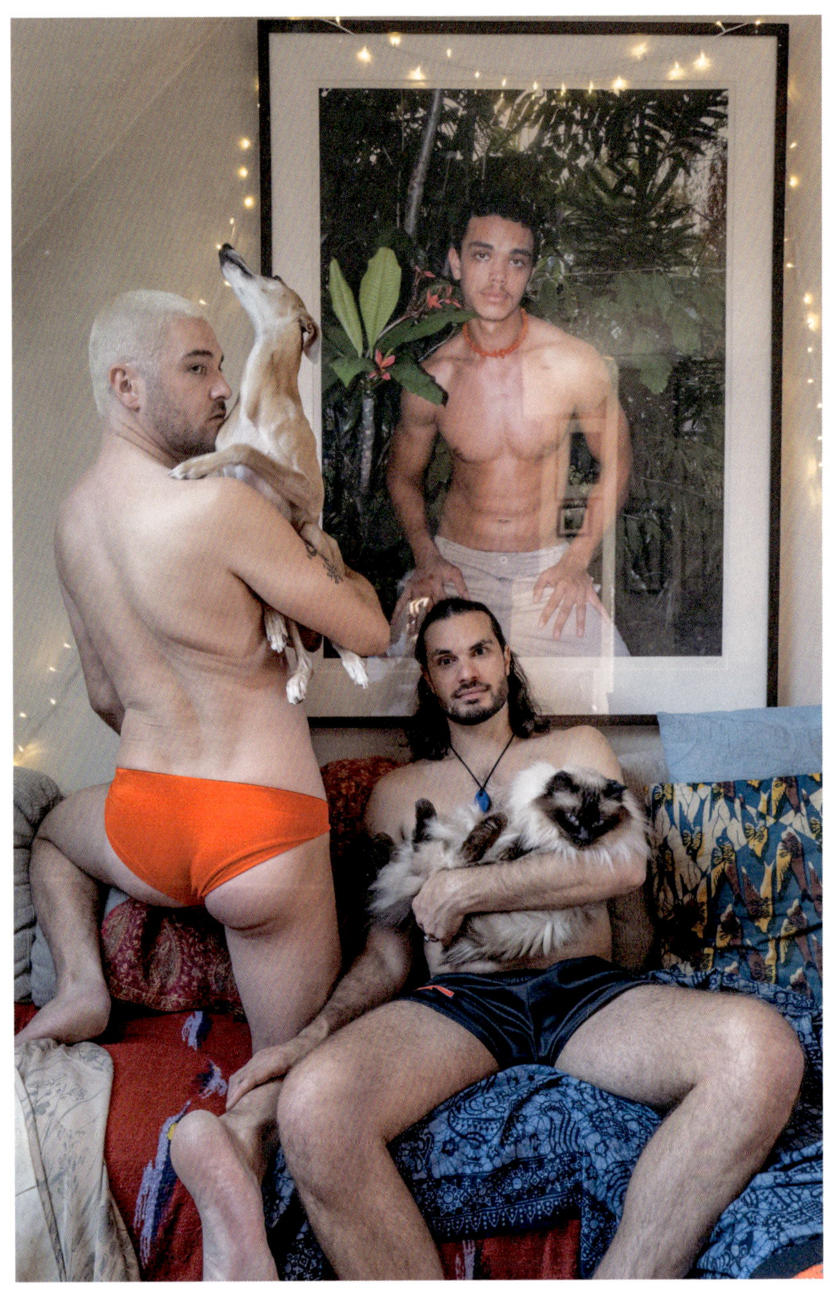

Myles and David 2024, from the series Lovers Revisited, Melbourne (made in collaboration with Charan Singh)

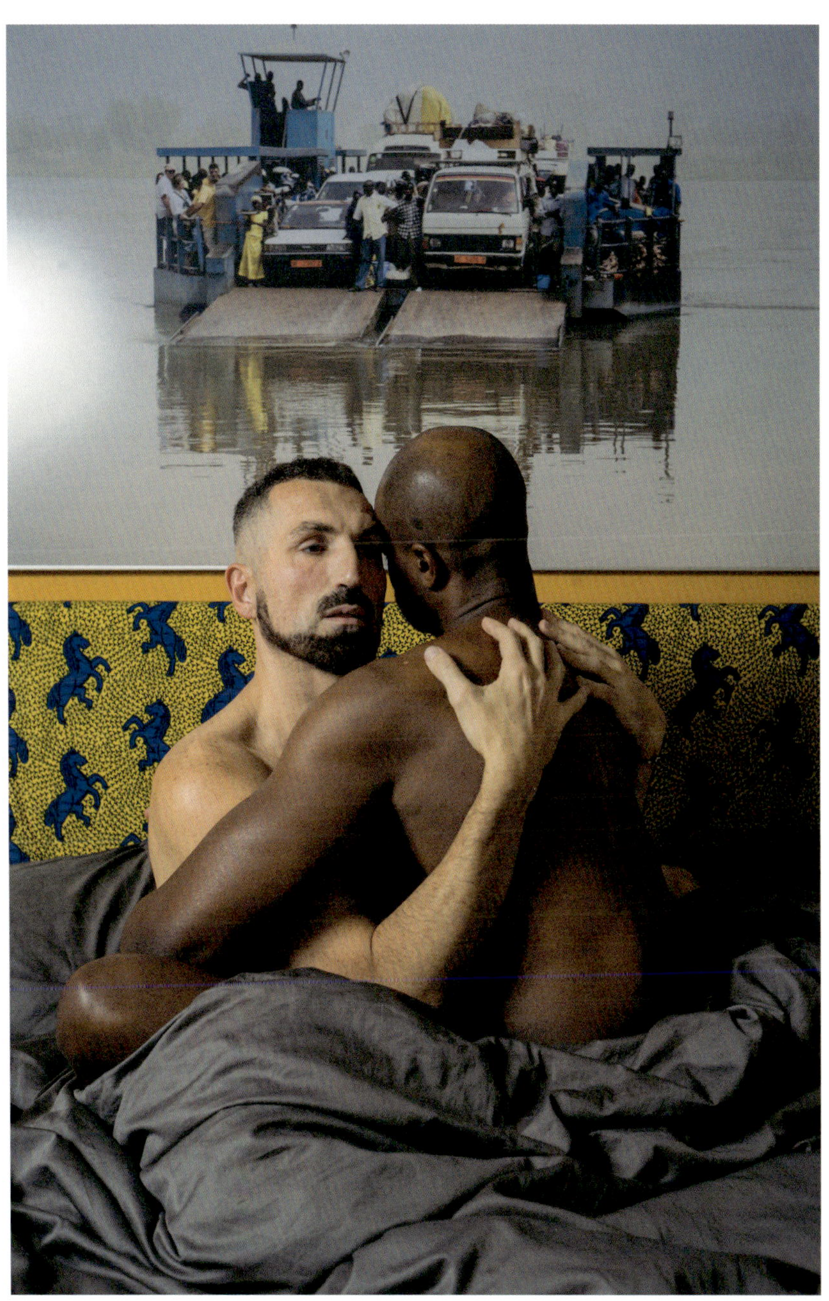

Nicola and Willy 2024, from the series Lovers Revisited, Paris (made in collaboration with Charan Singh)

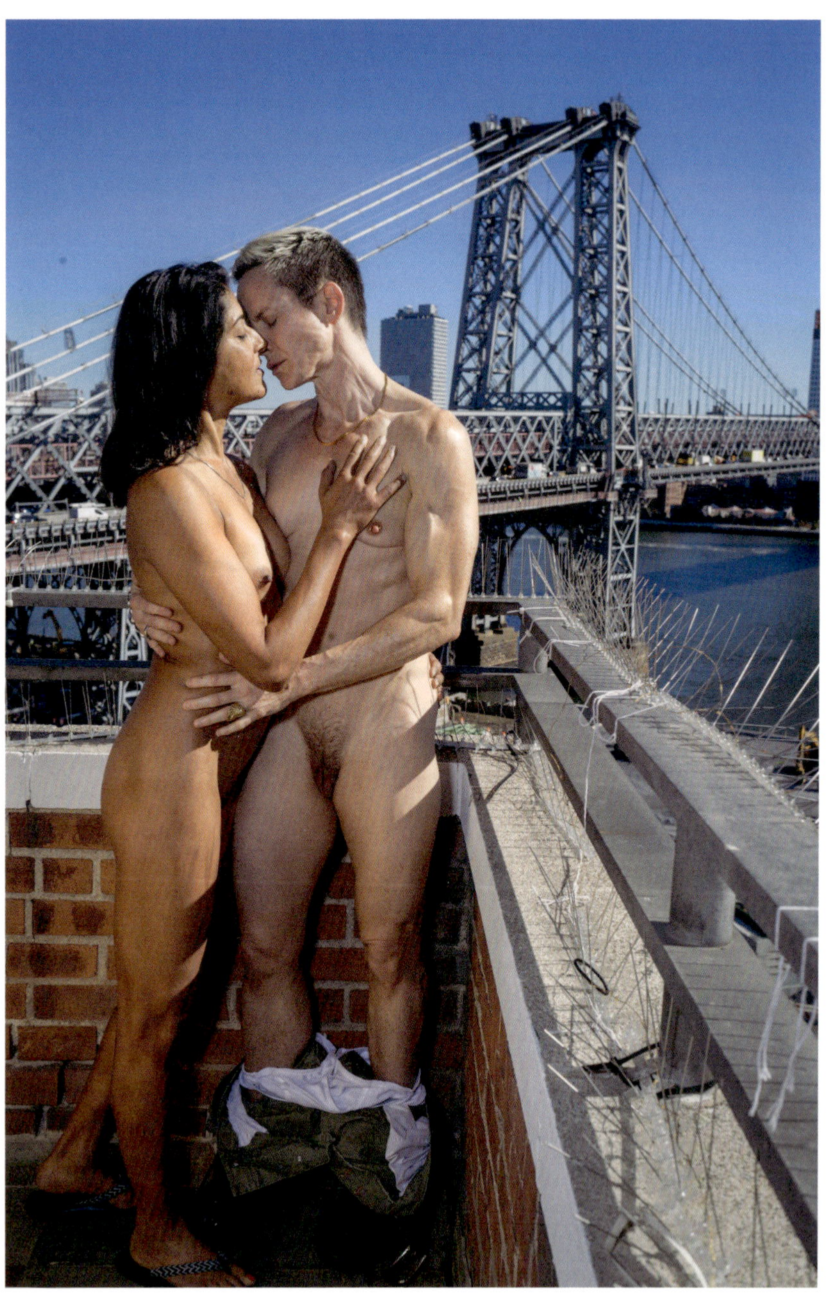

Gayatri and Cassils 2024, from the series Lovers Revisited, New York (made in collaboration with Charan Singh)

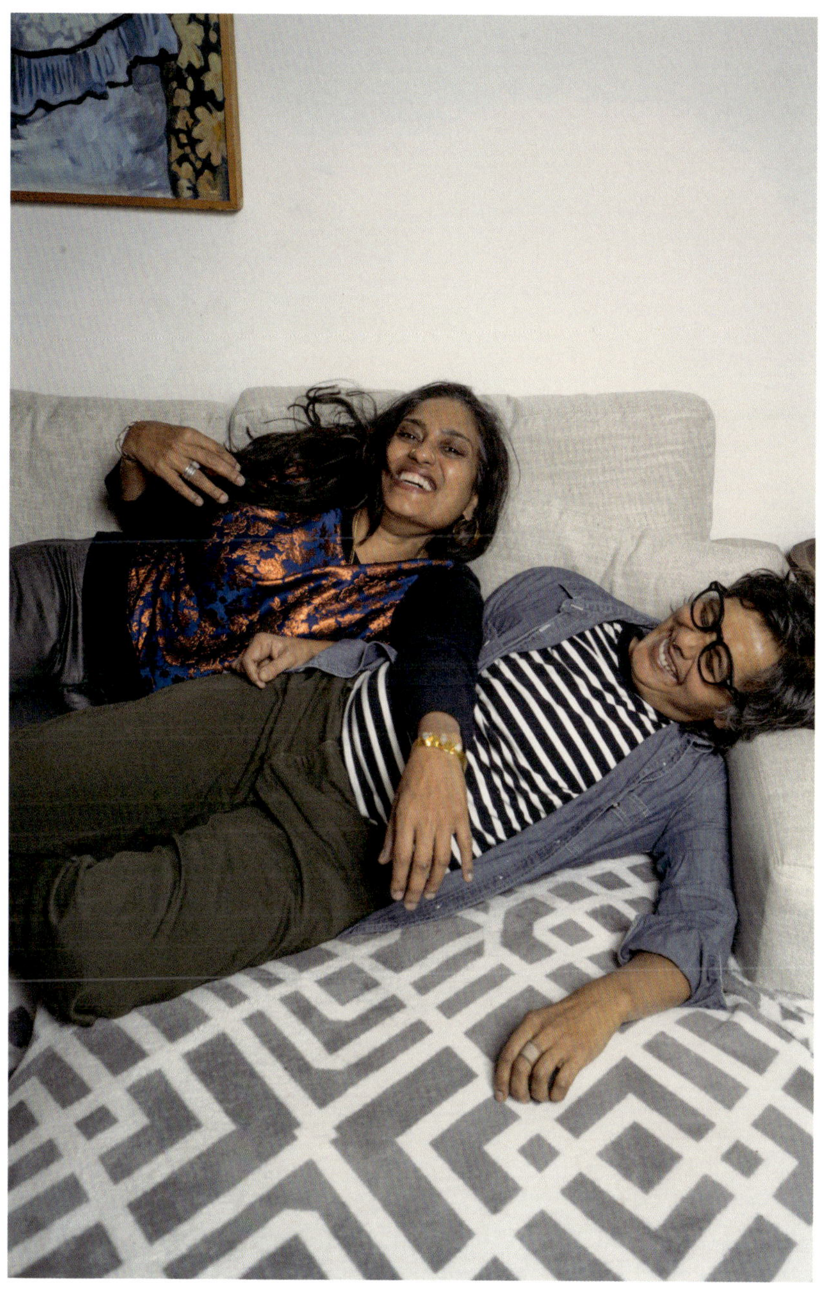

Chitra and Sva 2024, from the series Lovers Revisited, Brooklyn (made in collaboration with Charan Singh)

CREDITS

Photo credits
All images: Photo: Artimage 2025
Pages 47, 52–3, 55–7: Photo: Tate

ARTIST'S ACKNOWLEDGEMENTS

London
Charan Singh
Babe Gupta
Rudi Leuthold
Emily Andersen
Anna Fox
Steve Dodd
Monika Baker
Joy Gregory
Suraj Patel
Jesse Kahn
Elizabeth Lewis
John Hedgecoe
Eugenie Dodd
Mark Sealy
Roshini Kempadoo
Edward Ward
Chris Boot
Sue Davies
Tessa Boffin
Jean Fraser
Wendy Thomson

Montreal
Shalini Gupta
Penny and Ram Gupta
Fakroon Lakdawalla
Gerry French
Charles Fisch
Nikki Hussain
Glen Marcotte

New York
Lisette Model
Philippe Halsman
George Tice
Esa Epstein

Delhi
Radhika Singh
Chapal Mehra
Gauri Gill
Amit Jayaram
Aruna Roy
Saleem Kidwai
Roshini Vadehra
Vidya Shivadas
Deepti Sharma
Gautam Bhan
Mario d'Penha
Lesley Esteves
Jivi Sethi
Ranbir SIngh

Galleries
Vadehra Art Gallery, New Delhi
Hales, London & New York
Stephen Bulger Gallery, Toronto
Materià, Rome